SECURITY RISK MANAGEMENT AIDE-MEMOIRE

Julian Talbot

SERT Pty Ltd

GPO Box 5460

Sydney NSW 2001 Australia

Email: Julian@juliantalbot.com

Copyright © 2019 Julian Talbot

All rights reserved.

ISBN: 9780648690702 (Kindle)
ISBN: 9781695622739 (Paperback)

First edition 2019

Dedicated with thanks to the countless researchers and practitioners who developed the ideas in this book, and to the security and risk professionals who make the world a safer place.

INTRODUCTION ... 1
- Preface ... 1
- Objectives ... 2
- How to Use This Aide Memoire ... 3
- Software ... 4
- Contributors ... 5

PART A: CORE CONCEPTS ... 6
- Swiss-Cheese ... 7
- Bow-Tie Model ... 9
- Human Factors ... 10
- ALARP ... 20
- P2R2 ... ??
- DDDRR ... ??
- Hierarchy of Controls ... 24
- Root Cause Analysis ... 27
- Qualitative vs Quantitative Analysis ... 31

PART B: METHODOLOGY ... 32
- Security Risk Assessment ... 33
- Scope, Context, Criteria ... 37
- Assets/Resources at Risk ... 42
- Threat Assessment ... 46
- Controls ... 58
- Risk Identification ... 60
- Risk Registers ... 66

PART C: ADDITIONAL TOOLS ... 68
- The Right Tool For Each Job ... 69
- Threat Assessment Tools ... 71
- Intelligence Analysis ... 75
- Criticality Assessment ... 80
- Vulnerability Analysis ... 82
- Risk Analysis ... 85
- Risk Evaluation ... 114
- Risk Treatments ... 115
- Risk Communication ... 125
- Recording Observations ... 132
- Assessing the Quality of SRM ... 134

SRM Maturity Models ... 138
Enterprise Security Risk Assessment ... 143
SRA Project Brief Headings ... 145
SRA Report Headings ... 147
Security Plan Headings ... 150
Monte Carlo Simulation ... 152
Ishikawa Diagrams ... 153
Attack Trees ... 157

PART D: MODELS AND FRAMEWORKS ... 158
Definitions ... 159
ISO31000 Risk Management Standard ... 162
SRMBOK Framework ... 165
SRMBOK Methodology ... 169
Other Security Frameworks ... 172

PART E: REFERENCES ... 174

If You Like This Book ... 178
About the Author ... 179

INTRODUCTION

The Security Risk Management Aide-Memoire (SRMAM) is based on the Security Risk Management Body of Knowledge (SRMBOK), with some updates to include other material, new research, and the update of ISO31000 Risk Management Standard in 2018. I will keep updating it based on suggestions from readers and additional research, and I welcome any suggestions.

My intention was to produce a pocket guide but as you can see, there is a lot of ground to cover. SRMAM is as brief as I could make it, however it has also inspired me to start work on a longer, more comprehensive book on security risk assessment, which will expand on much of this material.

SRMAM is available in paperback and electronic versions from Amazon or free-of-charge when you set up a paid or free account with Sectara.com. Much of the content can also be found online at www.srmam.com where there is also a forum to ask questions and discuss some of the concepts. I will progressively add new material and explanatory videos at www.srmam.com.

If you would like to contribute to future editions you can post feedback or improvement suggestions in an Amazon review, or via www.juliantalbot.com.

Julian Talbot
October 2019

Objectives of this Aide-Memoire

This Security Risk Management Aide-Memoire (SRMAM) is designed as a memory jogger that security risk practitioners might find useful for typical activities such as conducting a security risk assessment, facilitating a workshop, drafting a report, etc.

The assumption in this booklet is that you are already at least somewhat familiar with all the tools and ideas outlined here, as well as the specific tools of your profession. The intention is to cover security risk management across all domains. You will not find much that is specific to cyber, people, information, or physical security, nonetheless this guide should be equally applicable in any of those domains. Most of the contents will also be applicable to any area of risk management. Specific technical tools such as engineering analysis, details about penetration testing, Monte Carlo simulation, Black-Scholes, etc. are outside the scope of this text. Entire books have been written about these topics.

With that caveat, most of the tools and models here are complementary. You can pick and choose the ones that work best for you. Some may be in conflict with each other or with existing corporate systems. Take what works for you and ignore the rest or keep it in your back pocket for possible later use.

Last but not least, I hope you find this Aide-Memoire useful but I leave you with the words of George Box:

"All models are wrong. Some are useful."

How to Use This Aide-Memoire

You can use this little booklet however you see fit, but here are a few suggestions.

1. It has been designed so that you can carry the concepts, taxonomies, diagrams, and concepts with you in your pocket or on your phone as a memory jogger.
2. The models, ideas, and graphics are also useful when you need to show them to someone you are working with, or share concepts and methods.
3. The diagrams and models can be helpful for presentations, training, brainstorming and briefings.
4. The models in this book are a starting point. You may notice what appear to be internal inconsistencies. This is so that you do not rely on a particular methodology or tool. The minor variations presented in some diagrams (eg: Swiss-Cheese, Human Factors(HFACS)) are designed to illustrate possibilities. Choose what works for you.

Being intended as a pocketbook, has made it difficult to offer the graphics in a reasonable size so I have made high resolution images and PowerPoint files available for viewing and download at www.srmam.com.

There is nothing mandatory in this book and no Standards were harmed or created in the process of compiling it. I encourage you to continue to modify and tailor these ideas, models, and diagrams for your own situation. And if you do make improvements, and would be interested in sharing them in a future edition of this booklet, please contact me via JulianTalbot.com.

Software

MS Excel has long been the go-to tool for creating security risk assessments, and I have explored just about every capability it has. There are, of course, other alternatives and risk assessment tools but none that have offered me enough to switch from Excel. Until now.

A friend has been working on a recently released Software-as-a-Service (SaaS) security risk assessment product which allows users to create professional and methodologically rigorous assessments, with all the benefits you would expect of a collaborative, secure and productivity-inducing platform.

SECTARA was developed by leading security risk practitioner Konrad Buczynski and his team. I have had the pleasure of having an ongoing level of involvement and interest. SECTARA puts into action SRMBOK concepts, in a way that makes it very easy to produce a professional report and security risk treatment plan.

Software of course will not make you a better security risk assessor (that's what this book is for right?) but it will save you some time when it comes to documenting and presenting a rigorous security risk assessment. And, I am pleased to announce that a fully featured version of SECTARA is available for free. There are paid plans for large organizations, but if you just need to conduct a few security risk assessments I think you will be pleasantly surprised by SECTARA.

Try out the free plan at your leisure (https://sectara.com/free-plan). If you are loyal to MS Excel, you can also check out my website at www.juliantalbot.com for some free templates.

Contributors

I would like to give my deepest thanks to the following people who have been so generous with their time and made major contributions to this book. These people are experts in their field. Many of them work as consultants and volunteer in professional associations so I encourage anyone who needs help with security risk management to reach out to them.

The following people have inspired, informed, or helped with this book so my thanks to Bruce Mateer, Chris Oxley, Craig Bain, Dave Van Lambaart, Gav Schneider, Jason Brown, Konrad Buczynski, Larry Clark, Mark Jarratt, Marty Smith, Matthew Curtis, Miles Jakeman, Nick Janicki, Paul Dunlop, Paul Longley, Stewart Hayes, Tony Ridley, and Tony Solomon.

Without your help, this would not be the book is it now. Any errors, as always, belong to me, but your support from within the security community has made this book a useful part of a toolbox for the security risk management professional. I would also like to thank my editor Julie-Anne Meaney for correcting my grammar and typos, and improving your experience of this book. You can find all the above as clickable links at srmam.fyi.to/contributors.

PART A: CORE CONCEPTS

Swiss-Cheese

Swiss-Cheese is a concept that for an event to occur, a number of 'holes' have to align in the barriers that are in place.[1]

PART A: CORE CONCEPTS

Swiss-Cheese Example

In this example, intelligence agents gain physical access to corporate servers and steal corporate data.

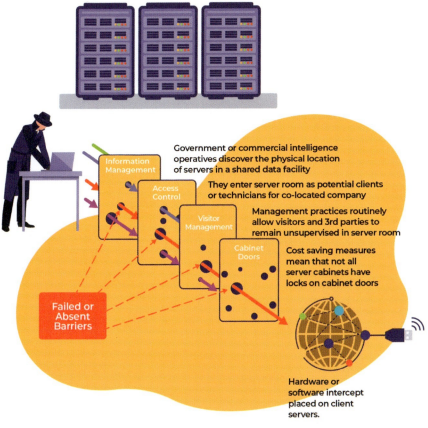

Government or commercial intelligence operatives discover the physical location of servers in a shared data facility

They enter server room as potential clients or technicians for co-located company

Management practices routinely allow visitors and 3rd parties to remain unsupervised in server room

Cost saving measures mean that not all server cabinets have locks on cabinet doors

Hardware or software intercept placed on client servers.

Customer and corporate records compromised.

NOTE: Most data breaches occur remotely via software vulnerabilities but a) this is a lot easier example for non-IT people and b) it is (sadly) a real world example.

Bow-Tie Model

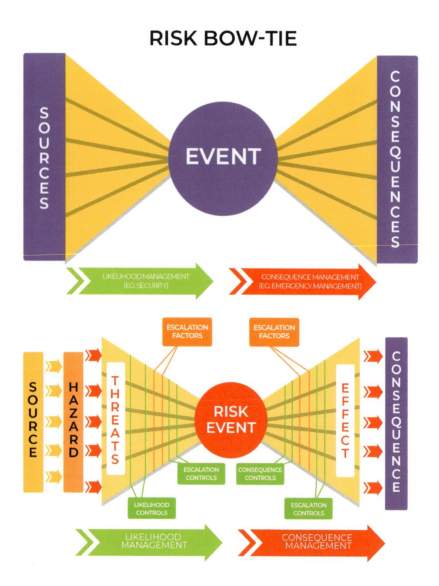

Human Factors

Core Concepts

Culture is the set of encouraged and acceptable behaviors, discussions, decisions and attitudes toward taking and managing risk within a group.

Automaticity is the term given by psychologists to the skilled action that people develop through repeatedly practicing the same activity, for example driving a car. Behaviors learned to the point of "automaticity" are not easily changed by conscious control.

High Reliability Organizations (HROs) are organizations that have succeeded in avoiding catastrophes in an environment where normal accidents can be expected, due to risk factors and complexity. Five characteristics of HROs have been identified as responsible for the "mindfulness" that keeps them working well when facing unexpected situations.

- Preoccupation with failure: HROs treat anomalies as symptoms of a problem with the system.
- Reluctance to simplify interpretations: HROs take deliberate steps to comprehensively understand the work environment as well as specific situations.
- Sensitivity to operations: HROs are continuously sensitive to unexpectedly changed conditions.
- Commitment to resilience: HROs develop the capability to detect, contain, and recover from errors.
- Deference to expertise: During a crisis, decisions are

made at the front line and authority migrates to the person who can solve the problem, regardless of their hierarchical rank.

Risk Homeostasis Theory (RHT) was nitially proposed by Gerald J.S. Wilde, a professor at Queen's University, Canada in 1982. RHT proposes that, for any activity, people accept a particular inbuilt level of subjectively-evaluated risk, in order to gain from a range of benefits associated with that activity. This level varies between individuals. When the level of acceptable risk in one part of the individual's life changes; there will be a corresponding rise/drop in acceptable risk elsewhere.

Sense-making is the process by which people give meaning to their collective experiences. It is the ongoing retrospective development of plausible images that rationalize what people are doing.

Culture is critical for risk management and would require several books in its own right. The following graphic however, is one approach that has worked for this author.

PART A: CORE CONCEPTS

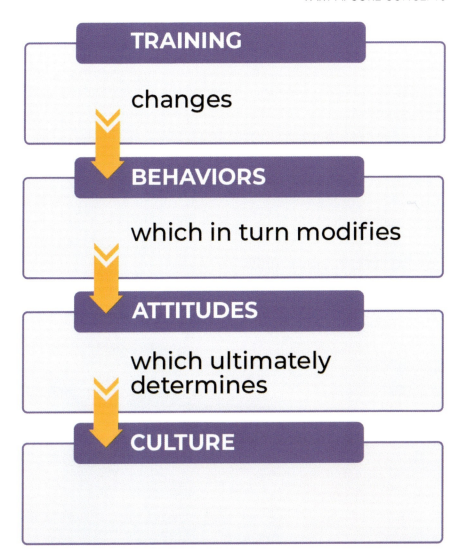

Bradley Curve

The DuPont™ Bradley Curve™ identifies four stages of safety culture maturity: Reactive, Dependent, Independent and Interdependent

1. Reactive Stage - People don't take responsibility and believe accidents will happen.
2. Dependent Stage - People view safety as following rules. Accident rates decrease.
3. Independent Stage - People take responsibility and believe they can make a difference with actions. Accidents reduce further.
4. Interdependent Stage - Teams feel ownership and responsibility for safety culture. They believe zero injuries is an attainable goal.

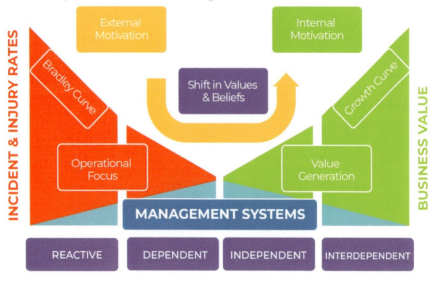

Heuristics and Biases

Rather than being the purely logical creatures we would like to believe, humans use shortcuts, rules of thumb, stereotypes, and biases; often known as "heuristics" to make decisions about risk. These heuristics affect how we think about risks, how we evaluate the probability and consequences of risk. They help us generate close-to-optimal answers quickly with limited information and effort. Heuristics are simple strategies to form judgments and make decisions by focusing on the most relevant aspects of a complex problem.[1]

Cognitive biases are systematic patterns of information-processing rules (mental shortcuts), called heuristics, that the brain uses to produce decisions or judgments. Dozens have been confirmed by research, with others likely to be discovered. Cognitive bias (e.g. mental noise) and motivational bias (e.g. when beliefs are distorted by wishful thinking) can be present at the same time.[2]

Daniel Kahneman uses the metaphor of two agents, called System 1 and System 2, which respectively produce fast (heuristic/intuitive) and slow (analytical/logical) thinking. In the picture that emerges from recent research, the intuitive System 1 is more influential than our experience tells us, and it is the secret author of many of the choices and judgments we make.[3]

Situational Awareness

Developing self-knowledge and situational awareness is a key element in providing individual or organizational security. These skills can be improved at the individual and organizational level by training to improve the following capabilities[1]:

- Maintain a level of observation of the surrounding environment.
- Evaluate and understand what may cause harm or be a threat.
- Assess the behavior and intentions of people in the environment.
- Determine whether there is anything suspicious or out of the ordinary.
- Have the knowledge, foresight and confidence to remove oneself from adverse situations before they develop or, in the worst case, manage incidents if they occur.
- Report observations to the relevant authorities.
- Possibly most importantly, to maintain a robust mental state of resilience.

OODA Loop

"He who can handle the quickest rate of change survives."

Lt. Colonel John Boyd

The OODA loop refers to the cycle Observe, Orient, Decide, Act.

It was developed by military strategist and United States Air Force Colonel John Boyd for the combat operations process. The approach explains how agility in decision making can overcome raw power in dealing with human opponents.

OODA loop refers to decision-making and the concept is to make better decisions, faster than your adversary, so that can act before they do and operate 'inside their OODA loop'.

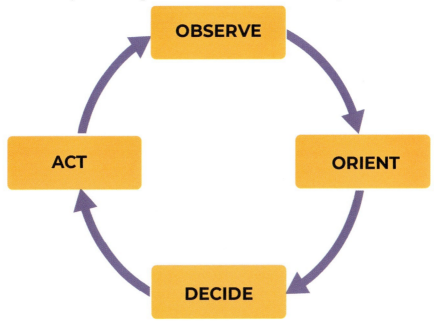

Human Factors Analysis Classification System

Human factors can cause a number of issues for risk management. The following graphics are adapted from the US Department of Defence Human Factors Analysis Classification System[1] (HFACS) 7.0 which is based on the work of James Reason[2]. HFACS offers a systemic taxonomy for categorizing and analyzing human errors.

Human Factors

ORGANIZATIONAL INFLUENCES

| Resource Problems | Personnel Selection & Staffing | Policy & Process Issues | Climate/Culture Issues |

SUPERVISION

| Supervisory Violations | Planned Inappropriate Operations | Inadequate Supervision |

PRE-CONDITIONS

Environment
-Physical Environment

-Technological Environment

Teamwork

Physical & Mental State
-Physical Problem
-State of Mind
-Sensory Misperception
-Mental Awareness

ACTS

| Performance Base Errors | Judgement & Decision Making Errors | Violations |

Security Risk Management Aide-Memoire

HFACS Example

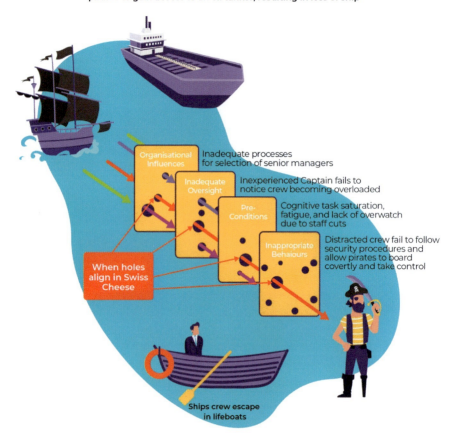

ALARP

ALARP stands for As Low As Reasonably Practicable. This term has been enshrined in UK case law since the case of Edwards v. National Coal Board in 1949.

The ruling was that the risk must be significant in relation to the sacrifice (in terms of money, time or trouble) required to avert it: risks must be averted unless there is a gross disproportion between the costs and benefits of doing so.

As Low as Reasonably Practicable (ALARP) is a level of risk that is tolerable and cannot be reduced further without expenditure of costs disproportionate to the benefit gained or where the solution is impractical to implement.

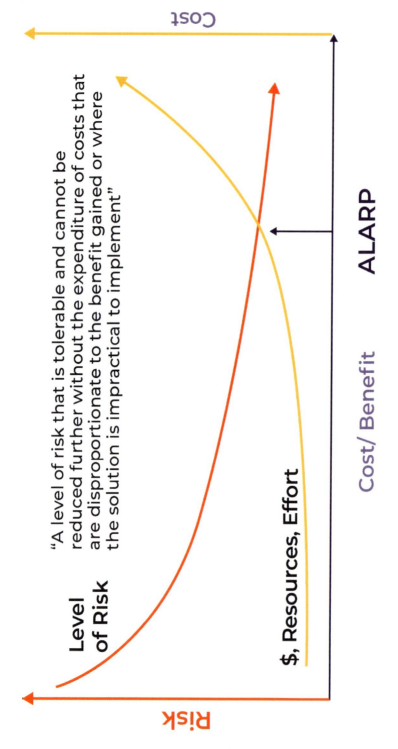

P2R2

P2R2 is an all-hazards approach for incident and emergency management. All stages can occur concurrently, albeit with a different focus at different stages, pre-event and post-event. There are variations on this but the following is a well known version.

- **Prevention** - take actions to reduce or eliminate the likelihood or effects of an incident. Learn more about preparing a risk management plan.

- **Preparedness** - take steps before an incident to ensure effective response and recovery. Read about conducting a business impact analysis.

- **Response** - contain, control or minimize the impacts of an incident. Learn more about preparing an incident response plan.

- **Recovery** - take steps to minimize disruption and recovery times. Read about developing a recovery plan.

DDDRR

Deter, Detect, Delay, Respond and Recover

DDD-RR Model

A series of barriers are in place to protect bank capital however if they all fail and thieves are successful, profits will be reduced.

Hierarchy of Controls

The hierarchy of controls is based on the concept that not all risk treatments are equally effective. In order of priority it is best to:
- Eliminate the risk.
- Substitute the source of the risk.
- Isolate the resources from the risk
- Engineer barriers to protect from the risk
- Administrative controls to protect resources
- Protective equipment when exposed to the risk

Security Risk Management Aide-Memoire

HIERARCHY OF CONTROLS

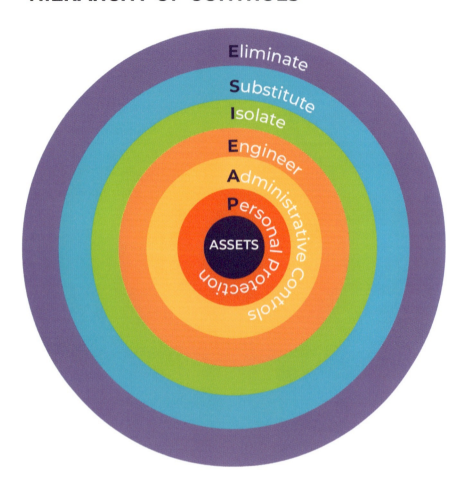

Hierarchy of Controls (ESIEAP)

Eg: Protection of Sensitive Information

E liminate	Shred or destroy all non-essential sensitive files
S ubstitute	Use open source information where suitable
I solate	Store all files in central location
E ngineer	Store files in security containers & under alarm
A dmin.	Security clearances, Training, Procedures, etc
P rotect	Protective markings on folders, lockable briefcases, etc.

Root Cause Analysis

Root Cause Analysis can be conducted in many ways but the essential elements involve starting with the event (actual or potential) and then considering what immediate causes might or did lead to the event. The next step is to consider the underlying root cause. The objective is to identify and mitigate the underlying root causes. For example, a security breach might have been caused but a faulty CCTV camera. The root cause however might trace back to a cut in maintenance budgets five years previously.

The following examples illustrate how a complex analysis of an incident can be summarized and presented in a single diagram. The first two diagrams are two halves of a single diagram, separated here for clarity.

In the first diagram, a hypothetical release of nerve gas on a subway starts from the event in the centre of the diagram. The immediate causes are shown on the left, then leading back to the underlying root cause and vulnerabilities. Directly to the left of each of these root causes are potential remedial actions. The causes and treatments have also been grouped in terms of their practice areas (Information, ICT, Physical Security, etc.) as shown on the far left.

The second diagram, illustrates the post-event (right hand side of the event). Immediate consequences have been plotted, along with the root causes of those consequences, and then recommended remedial actions. The diagram highlights the complexity of causation as most immediate causes have multiple root causes.

The third diagram plots the same hypothetical example using the HFACS framework to highlight four levels of causation.

See also: Human Factors(HFACS), Ishikawa Diagrams, Swiss-Cheese, DDDRR, and Human Factors(HFACS).

Enlarged versions of the following diagrams and templates can be found at www.srmam.com.

Security Risk Management Aide-Memoire

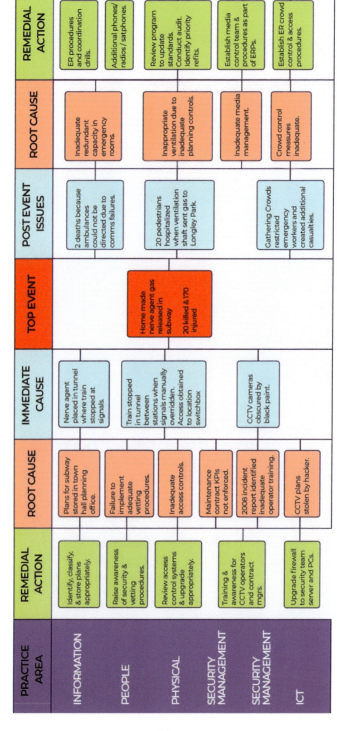

PART A: CORE CONCEPTS

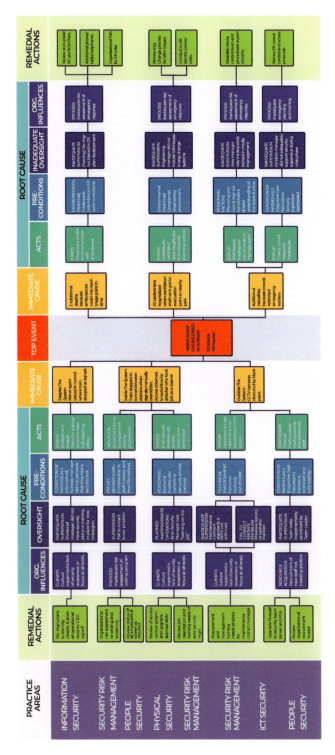

Qualitative vs Quantitative Analysis

Risk is usually described and analyzed using one of three approaches:
- **Qualitative:** Low, Medium, High or a similar descriptive ranking. (See for example: Threat Tolerance)
- **Semi-quantitative:** This might take the form of an ordinal ranking such as a 1 to 5 scale with some form of descriptive overview of broad categorization (Eg: $10,000 to $100,000 or 25% to 50%). See: Likelihood And Consequence Tables.
- **Quantitative:** This is often expressed as a ratio, percentage, 0.0 to 1.0 for probability calculation, frequencies (eg: lost time injuries per 100,000 person-hours worked), financial amounts, or similar quantitative data.

PART B: METHODOLOGY

Security Risk Assessment

ISO31000 Process

The key stages of the security risk management process (as per ISO31000:2018) are:
- Scope, Context, and Criteria
- Risk Assessment, which comprises 3 elements:
  - Risk Identification
  - Risk Analysis
  - Risk Evaluation
- Risk Treatment
- Monitoring and Review
- Recording and Reporting
- Communication and Consultation

Note: Monitoring and Review, Recording, and Reporting, and Communication and Consultation, are typically considered to be continual and concurrent practices. This means that they can occur at the same time, and run constantly throughout the risk assessment.

Scope, Context, Criteria, Risk Assessment, and Risk Treatment, may be one-off as part of a risk assessment or, ideally may be conducted continuously.

PART B: METHODOLOGY

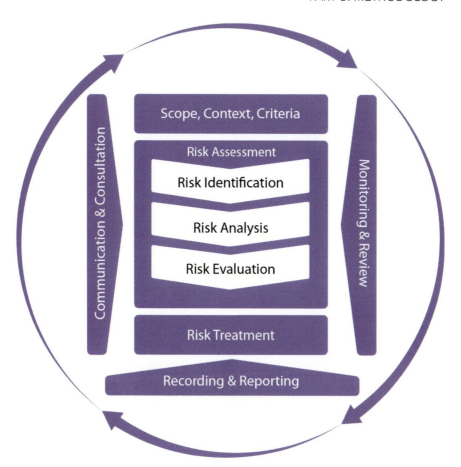

SRA and ISO31000

There are many ways to conduct a Security Risk Assessment (SRA). The graphics below are adapted from ISO31000:2018 Risk Management Standard.

Security Risk Assessment

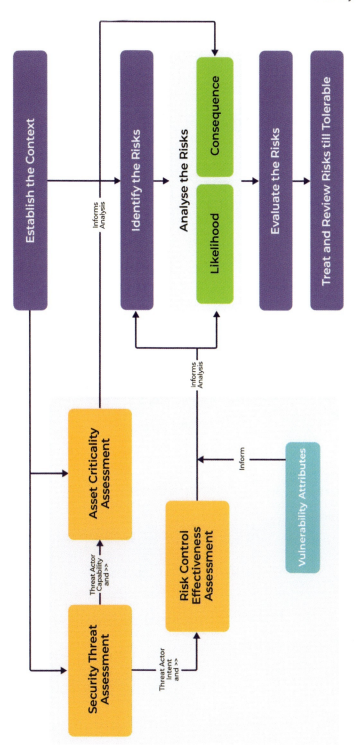

Scope, Context, Criteria

Scope

Scope considerations include:
- Objectives
- Expected outcomes
- Timeframe for analysis
- Geographic and virtual locations
- Business units to be included
- Inclusions and exclusions including practice areas and domains (eg: physical, ICT, safety, finance/fraud, etc.)
- Risk analysis tools and techniques
- Resources
- Responsibilities
- Records to be kept
- Relationships to other groups
- Projects, processes and activities.

Context

External and internal context combine to make up the environment in which the organization seeks to achieve its objectives.

External Context

PESTLE is a useful mnemonic to consider external context:
- Political influences such as legislation, trade tariffs, policy changes.
- Economic factors, both global and local.
- Social influences, expectations, trends, and demographics.
- Technological changes and implications.
- Legal environment and requirements for compliance, etc.
- Environmental factors such as pollution, climate change, stakeholder expectations, etc.

Internal Context

MORTAR is another useful mnemonic to help establish internal context:
- Management systems: policies, procedures, processes,
- Organization: culture, objectives, vision, ethics
- Resources: capabilities, cashflow, people, property, information, intellectual property
- Technologies: robotics, information, communication,
- Accountability: structure, ownership, governance
- Relationships: stakeholders, interconnections, dependencies

When analyzing internal context, SWOT analysis can also be helpful:

- Strengths of the organization
- Weaknesses of the organization
- Opportunities that may present themselves
- Threats to achievement of objectives

Criteria

Risk criteria include:
- The amount and type of risk the organization may or may not take
- Obligations and views of the stakeholders
- Uncertainties that can affect outcomes and objectives
- How we will measure and define likelihood and consequences
- Timeframe and time-related factors
- Measurement techniques and metrics
- How the level of risk is to be determined
- How combinations and sequences of multiple risks will be taken into account
- The organization's capacity and resources.

Ref: Risk Analysis (PART C: ADDITIONAL TOOLS)

Defining Risk Tolerance

Risk Tolerance can be articulated in whichever way is appropriate for each organization. The following is just one example.

RATING	SCORE	ACTION
VERY HIGH	9, 10	Immediate action required by the Executive Leadership
HIGH	7, 8	Urgent senior management attention needed
MEDIUM	6	Management responsibility must be specified
LOW	4, 5	Manage by routine procedures
VERY LOW	2, 3	Monitor

The Australian Government Department of Finance recommend the following 10-step process for defining risk appetite and tolerance:[1]

1. Appoint a core reference group
2. Validate current risk categories
3. Review current risk profile
4. Build a risk appetite statement template
5. Interview senior executive and define risk appetite statement
6. Engage with SME's to build and refine risk tolerance statements
7. Senior executive review
8. Amend risk appetite and tolerance statements as required
9. Committee Validation
10. Incorporate and communicate

Assets/Resources at Risk

Resources and assets can be categorized and defined to suit the organization's requirements.

Asset Groups
- Employees & Contractors
- Visitors
- Brand & Reputation
- Finances
- Buildings & Equipment
- Technology

Asset Categories
- Intangible
- Tangible
- Operational
- Utilities
- Personnel
- Infrastructure

PIPER

PIPER can be a helpful mnemonic for categorizing assets.

People
- Staff
- Stakeholders
- Visitors

Information
- Intellectual Property
- Data
- Records

Property
- Buildings
- Equipment
- Communications Technology

Economic
- Revenue and Income
- Capital
- Contingent Capital (eg: insurance)

Reputation
- Brand
- Media attention
- Social Media

Critical Infrastructure Protection (CIP)

Critical infrastructure is a term used by governments to describe assets that are essential for the functioning of a society and economy. Many organizations and nations have a critical infrastructure protection program.

The US National Infrastructure Protection Plan (NIPP) defines the following 16 critical infrastructure sectors:
- Chemical
- Commercial facilities
- Communications
- Critical manufacturing
- Dams
- Defence industrial base
- Emergency services
- Energy
- Financial services
- Food and agriculture
- Government facilities
- Healthcare and public health
- Information technology
- Nuclear reactors, materials, and waste
- Transportation systems
- Water and wastewater systems

The Australian Government Critical Infrastructure Centre defines eight critical infrastructure sectors:
- Banking and finance
- Government
- Communications
- Energy
- Food and grocery
- Health

Security Risk Management Aide-Memoire

- Transport
- Water

Threat Assessment

Sources of risk vary depending on whether you are analyzing a strategic, operational, or tactical situation. Individuals and organizations that do not have access to professional or classified government threat assessments should consider commercial sources or specialist consultants to help develop comprehensive and timely threat assessments.

Detailed threat analysis methodology is not addressed in this book, however the key issue is that a Threat Assessment (TA) is used by the decision maker or security analyst to make informed decisions with an understanding of the threat environment. A poorly developed Threat Assessment reduces the overall credibility of the security risk assessment.

The following pages and Threat Assessment Tools in PART C: ADDITIONAL TOOLS provide an overview of the key elements and approaches for developing threat assessments.

Sources of Risk

Sources of Risk can include any number of elements, however they can broadly be considered as:
1. Threat Actors (Criminals, Hackers, etc.)
2. Hazards (Explosives, Technology, etc.)

Threat Actors

Sources of risk (Threat Actors) can come from a multitude of sources. However, the following broad categories can be a useful framework for analyzing sources of risk in a consistent fashion.

NOTE: There is an inherent limitation in seeking to definitively categorize Threat Actors. These individuals and groups often fit into several categories. Examples include an Insider who commits a serious crime being concurrently part of a Serious Organized Criminal (SOC) group, or an Issue Motivated Group (IMG) who demonstrates the behaviour of a Petty Criminal etc.

- Trusted Insiders (TIs)
- Petty Criminals (PCs)
- Organized Criminals (OCs)
- Cybercriminals
- Terrorists
- Issue Motivated Groups (IMGs)
- State Intelligence Services (SISs)
- Commercial Espionage Services (CISs)

Hazards

Some examples of potential hazards which could be used by Threat Actors.

- Explosives (e.g. Improvised Explosive Devices)
- Technology (e.g. Pineapple Tetra)
- Radio frequency jammer
- Unsecured microphones and cameras
- Weapons (e.g. Guns, knives, etc.)

- Software (e.g. hacking software, ransomware)
- Hardware (e.g. electronic listening devices, keystroke loggers)
- Nuclear (e.g. nuclear bombs or material)
- Biological (e.g. White powder)
- Radiological (e.g. radioactive 'dirty bombs')
- Chemical weapons
- Staff incompetence (e.g. inadequate IT security training)
- Financial instruments (e.g. Fraudulent invoices)

Threat Assessment

Intent & Capability

Threat can be evaluated as a combination of Intent & Capability.

CAPABILITY \ INTENT	None	Little	Expressed	Determined	Dedicated
Extensive	S	H	E	E	E
Advanced	S	S	H	E	E
Developed	M	S	S	H	E
Moderate	L	M	S	S	H
Low	L	L	M	S	S

Legend:
- L — Low
- M — Moderate
- S — Significant
- H — High
- E — Extreme

Intent and Capability both comprise other elements as illustrated below.

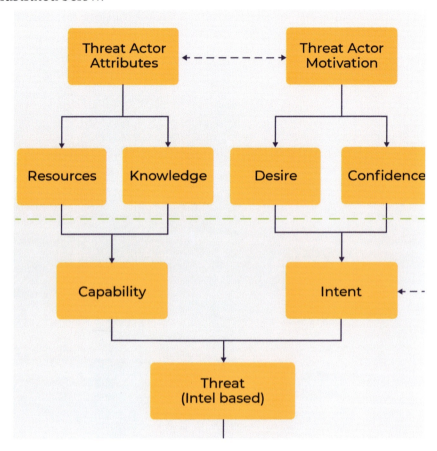

Assessing Threat

Threats can be assessed in many ways. However, one approach is to develop an ordinal ranking of Threat Actors' resources, knowledge, desires, and confidence (a.k.a. Expectance) to develop an overall threat profile.

Resources
What resources (or access to resources) does the attacker have at their disposal?

1. Few if any resources and/or funding
2. Limited funding and/or resources
3. Moderate level of financing and/or resources
4. Significant level of funding and/or resources.
5. Fully funded and resourced.

Knowledge

How much knowledge or skills does the attacker have?
1. No knowledge or training
2. Limited knowledge and ability.
3. Moderate level of training and skills.
4. Very skilled and trained in the use of tactics and techniques
5. Highly skilled and comprehensively trained.

Desire

What does the attacker desire?
1. Little to no desire - absence of drive and purpose
2. Some drive and commitment to achieve outcomes using generally peaceful means.
3. Highly motivated but with some flexibility in terms of method and capacity for compromise.
4. High degree of desire with limited room for compromise and potential to use extreme measures.
5. Extremist motivations with few if any limitations on attack options and no room for compromise.

Confidence (Expectance)

An attacker's confidence or expectation, can be ranked as follows:
1. Threat actor does not believe they have the capacity & competence to achieve an attack.
2. Threat actor believes they have limited capacity & competence to achieve an attack.

3. Threat actor has reasonable expectation of a successful attack based on their capacity & competence.

4. Threat actor competence and capabilities are such that they have high expectations of achieving a successful attack.

5. Threat actor has very high expectation of achieving a successful attack.

An example of the summary of a threat assessment is presented in the following graphic. This is NOT a Threat Assessment, merely the summary of potentially many pages of material and hours or months of research and analysis.

Threat Assessment

ID Category Threat Actors		T1
		Foreign Intelligence Services
		State Sponsored Commercial Espionage Groups
Attributes	Resources	These groups are generally highly resourced and well funded.
		5. Fully funded and resourced.
	Knowledge	Significant actors in this arena are usually extensively trained and have access to reliable intelligence.
		5. Highly skilled and comprehensively trained.
	CAPABILITY	A very capable and well prepared adversary with high tolerance for risk but with almost always operating covertly.
		5
Motivation	Desire	Aggressively seeking classified or related intelligence via any and all means.
		4. High degree of desire with limited room for compromise and potential to use extreme measures.
	Confidence	This group have a high level of confidence that over a sufficiently long time frame they will be successful in at least a significant number of their endeavours.
		4. Threat actor competence and capabilities are such that they have high expectations of achieving a successful attack.
	INTENT	Economic advantage over our Organization or on the world stage.
		4
THREAT		4.5

Threat Acts

Threat Acts (Events) are unlimited in range, variety, and significance but may include the following. They are listed here as physical or virtual attacks but it is important to recognize that many of them can fit into either.

Physical
- Armed attack
- Armed robbery
- Arson
- Assault
- Improvised explosive device (IED) attack
- Kidnap and ransom
- Malicious damage
- Non-violent protest
- Theft
- Trespass
- Vehicular attack
- Violent protest
- Workplace violence

Virtual
- Commercial espionage
- Compromise of electronic device
- Creation and distribution of a virus
- Cyberstalking
- Disclosure of sensitive information
- Distributed denial of service (DDOS) attack
- Electronic audio surveillance
- Electronic communications surveillance

- Electronic interception
- Fraud
- Identity theft
- Industrial espionage
- Malware
- Man-in-the-middle attack
- Network penetration
- Phishing
- Ransomware
- Social media campaign
- Theft of intellectual property

Threat Tolerance

Extreme	Threat Acts rated at this level will be the subject of formal individual Threat Assessments and carried forward to the Threat or Risk Register
High	Threat Acts rated at this level will be carried forward to the Threat or Risk Register and considered for individual or collective Threat Assessments.
Significant	Threat Acts rated at this level will be included in the Threat Register and considered for Threat Assessments.
Moderate	Threat Acts rated at this level will be recorded and monitored.
Low	Threat Acts at this level will be noted and evaluated to assess requirement for ongoing monitoring.

Controls

Adequacy of Existing Controls

The 'adequacy' score is intended to provide an insight into the operational effectiveness of existing systems to manage security risks. This assessment does not however, audit the individual controls in detail, other than to identify presenting security weaknesses.

Existing controls are considered in terms of the following 3 parameters to develop a qualitative assessment of their adequacy. Taking an average of the three (policy, assurance, compliance) can provide an overall rating of effectiveness.

METRIC	DESCRIPTION
POLICY	Policies, procedures and documented controls
ASSURANCE	Resourcing, capability and audit
COMPLIANCE	Implementation of Policy and Assurance measures

The following scoring system can provide a qualitative assessment of the adequacy of existing security controls against perceived risk. Note: A score of 5 might suggest the possibility of diverting costs or resources elsewhere while still achieving adequate risk management in this area.

Security Risk Management Aide-Memoire

DESCRIPTOR	SCORE	DESCRIPTION
NONE	1	Inadequate, identifies significant gaps which require immediate attention.
MINIMAL	2	Inadequate in some areas or circumstances. Identifies some notable gaps, which requires attention.
MODERATE	3	Adequate in most conditions. The system will be able to manage events effectively in most situations, however some improvement is required for improvement.
STRONG	4	Adequate in current conditions, with appropriate cost/benefit balance.
EXTENSIVE	5	More than adequate, in all foreseeable, likely circumstances.

Risk Identification

Strategies for Identifying Risks

Techniques for identifying risks include:
- Incident Report Analysis
- Documentation Reviews
- Brainstorming
- Delphi Technique
- Red Teaming
- Intelligence Reports
- Threat Assessments
- Interviews
- Root Cause Analysis
- Swot Analysis (Strengths, Weaknesses, Opportunities And Threats)
- Checklist Analysis (eg: PESTLE, SERCL, Audit Instruments)
- Assumption Analysis
- Work Breakdown Structure

SERCL

Security events are not the ideal way to discover and document your 'unknown-unknowns'. Tools such as '**SERCL**' can be a useful mnemonic for identifying risks in advance.

- Source(s): Relevant source(s) of risk?
- Event: The single key event that might be evident if this threat occurs.
- Resource(s): Resources or assets likely to be targeted or impacted.
- Consequence(s): Likely effect on Resources and/or Objectives.
- Likelihood: The probability that the event will occur.

It may be useful in many circumstances to consider them in the following order:

1. Resources/Assets at risk
2. Sources of risk
3. Events which might occur
4. Likelihood of attack / event
5. Consequences (effect on objectives)

Not all sources of risk will involve every resource or risk event, e.g. hackers are unlikely to steal a building; but developing a list for each of S, E, & R then adding likely consequences is a good start.

The following graphic highlights how the five elements of SERCL fit within the ISO31000 Process.

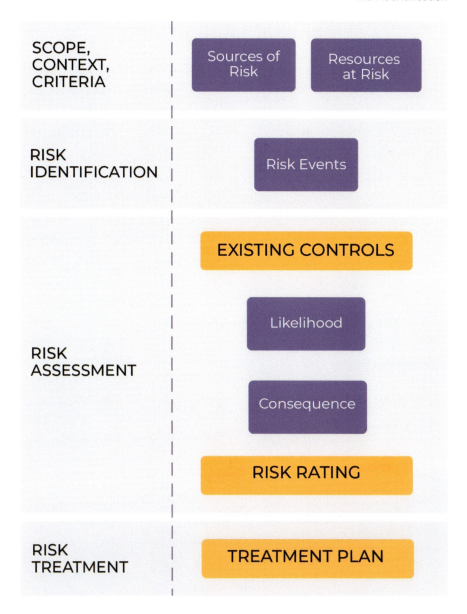

Elements of a Risk Statement

It may be helpful to build lists of assets that could be affected. These are potential Sources, Events, Resources that are at risk and the consequences incurred if they are breached. Linking them to create plausible scenarios can help to create risk statements.

Some examples:

- Compromise of sensitive information (*Resource*) due to untrained staff (*Source*) inadvertently posting incorrect files to a public website (*Event*) causing competitive disadvantage and resulting in financial losses (*Consequence*).
- IED Attack (*Event*) by Terrorists (*Source*) on one of our offices in Europe (*Resource*) causing multiple deaths (*Consequence*).

SOURCE	EVENT	RESOURCE	CONSEQUENCE
Competitors	Espionage	Information	Financial
Organized Criminals	Espionage	Information	Financial
Untrained Staff	Unauthorized Release	Information	Reputation
Organized Criminals	Theft	Equipment	Capability
Petty Criminals	Theft	Equipment	Financial

Risk Identification

Risk ID	Risk No. 5
Event	Espionage
Source	Competitors
Resource	Information
Consequence	Financial
Cons. Rating	Moderate
L'hood Rating	Likely
RISK RATING	HIGH

How To Write A Risk Statement

There is no set way to write a risk statement but there several pitfalls that can be easily avoided.

A one-word risk statement such as 'Terrorism' or a phrase such as 'Hackers accessing our network' will prove difficult if not impossible, to establish agreement regarding its rating or priority.

When expressing negative risks, it can be useful to start with the term "Failure to…", "Limited…" or "Loss of…". For example:

- Failure to protect Sensitive information (IP, intel reports, policy, etc.) from Foreign Intelligence Services exploiting audio and visual surveillance equipment.
- Limited operating capital may lead to a lack of investment in security R&D with resulting negative impact on our objectives.
- Loss of revenue due to reliance on a single large installation which is vulnerable to physical attack may have negative impact on our objectives.

Similarly, positive risk can be expressed by using "… offers an opportunity to…" or "Potential to…". For example:

- Our experience with our corporate security operations center offers an opportunity to expand our managed services offerings and improve our finances.
- Potential to operate in high-risk offshore environments more safely and at a lower cost than our competitors, due to our security team's international experience.

Risk Registers

Example of Headings - Risk Register

The following column headings are one example of how to structure a risk register to include recommended risk treatments.

- ID
- Threats
- Asset at Risk
- Risk Controls
- Risk Description
- Risk Type
- Current Risk
- Recommended Treatments
- Residual Risk

Example of Headings - Complex Risk Register

- Risk ID number
- Risk
- Category
- Asset/resource most likely at risk
- Description of Risk
- Adequacy of Existing Controls
    - Policy
    - Assurance
    - Compliance
    - Overall Control Rating
- Current Risk
    - Likelihood
    - Consequence
    - Risk Rating
- Treatments
    - Treatment ID numbers
    - Treatment Notes
- Residual Risk Rating

PART C: ADDITIONAL TOOLS

The Right Tool For Each Job

When security risk assessments start to get too complex or time consuming, it is usually because the wrong tool is being applied to the job. As security risk professionals, we need a range of tools to suit the size of the task at hand. Here are a few examples in increasing level of complexity.

- **TAKE 2** - Simply *take 2 minutes* to think before undertaking a potentially risky behavior, such as walking down a dark alleyway or pressing 'Send' on that email
- **STEP BACK 5 x 5** - Physically or mentally *step back 5 meters* and take 5 minutes to discuss what could go wrong with, for example, this server patch upload, or business trip.
- **JOB HAZARD ANALYSIS (JHA)** - are a structured one-page analysis tool, which breaks down the activity into a series of steps and considers the risks and potential mitigations involved in each individual task or activity.
- **PROJECT RISK PLAN** - involves more complex risk modeling, such as, Monte Carlo simulations and formal risk registers.
- **DETAILED RISK ASSESSMENT** - refers to a formal documented process of developing a risk register and risk treatment plan (e.g. as per ISO31000)
- **COMPLEX RISK ASSESSMENTS** - are resource intensive and only warranted for significant high risk activities and or enterprise-level security risk assessments.

PART C: ADDITIONAL TOOLS

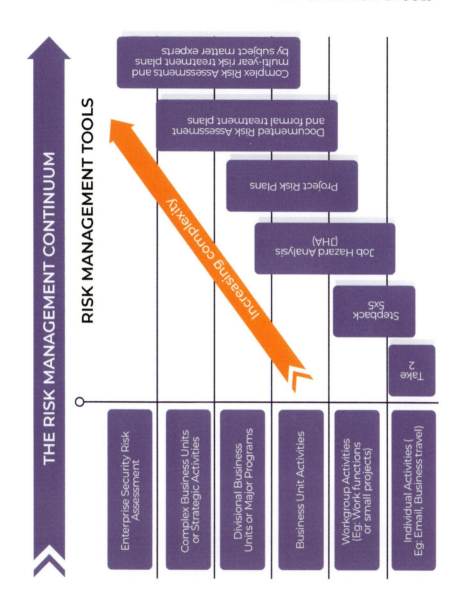

Threat Assessment Tools

Attacker Perspective

When considering how various attackers might view your organization, it may be helpful to plot them on a matrix like this.

Attacker's Perspective of Target

Attractiveness ↑	**OPPORTUNITY** Seek opportunities and fresh weaknesses. Maintain loose watching brief	**PRIMARY TARGET** Seek opportunities and fresh weaknesses. Conduct surveillance to assess vulnerabilities, prepare resources and develop plan of attack.
	AVOID Give low attention Bypass without loss	**SECONDARY** Monitor for changes in suitability.
	Ability →	

Defender Perspective

When considering multiple sources of risk, it may help to categorize and prioritize them based on the attributes of the attacker.

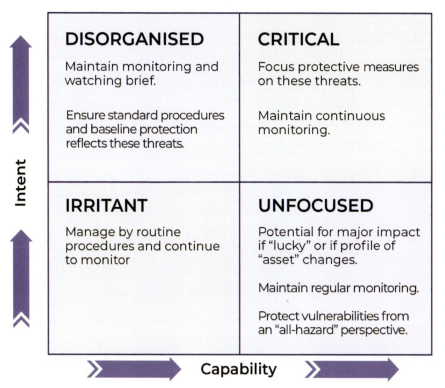

Security Content Automation Protocol (SCAP)

SCAP is a method for using specific standards to enable automated vulnerability management, measurement, and policy compliance evaluation, e.g. FISMA compliance.[1] The National Vulnerability Database (NVD) is the U.S. government content repository for SCAP.[2]

The SCAP suite of specifications standardize the nomenclature and formats used by these automated vulnerability management, measurement, and policy compliance products.

Components of SCAP include:

- Common Vulnerabilities and Exposures (CVE) - a naming system for describing security vulnerabilities.
- Common Configuration Enumeration (CCE) - a naming system for system configuration issues.
- Common Vulnerability Scoring System (CVSS) - a standardized scoring system for describing the severity of security vulnerabilities.
- Common Platform Enumeration (CPE) - a standardized method of describing and identifying classes of applications, operating systems, and hardware devices.
- Extensible Configuration Checklist Description Format (XCCDF) - an XML format specifying security checklists, benchmarks and configuration documentation.
- Open Vulnerability and Assessment Language (OVAL) - a language for describing security testing procedures.

STRIDE

STRIDE is a model of threats developed by Praerit Garg and Loren Kohnfelder at Microsoft for identifying computer security threats.[1] It provides a mnemonic for security threats in six categories (threatened attributes are in brackets). The threats are:

- Spoofing of user identity (Authenticity)
- Tampering (Integrity)
- Repudiation (Non-repudiability)
- Information disclosure / privacy breach or data leak (Confidentiality)
- Denial of service (Availability)
- Elevation of privilege (Authorization)

Intelligence Analysis

Admiralty Scale

The Admiralty System or NATO System is a method for evaluating collected items of intelligence. It consists of a two-character notation, evaluating the reliability of the source and the assessed level of confidence on the information.

Reliability of Source

A source is assessed for reliability based on a technical assessment of its capability, or in the case of Human Intelligence sources, their history. The notation uses Alpha coding, A-F:

A. Completely reliable: No doubt of authenticity, trustworthiness, or competency; has a history of complete reliability

B. Usually reliable: Minor doubt about authenticity, trustworthiness, or competency; has a history of valid information most of the time

C. Fairly reliable: Doubt of authenticity, trustworthiness, or competency but has provided valid information in the past

D. Not usually reliable: Significant doubt about authenticity, trustworthiness, or competency but has provided valid information in the past

E. Unreliable: Lacking in authenticity, trustworthiness, and competency; history of invalid information

F. Reliability cannot be judged: No basis exists for

evaluating the reliability of the source

Credibility

An item is assessed for credibility based on likelihood and levels of corroboration by other sources. The notation uses a numeric code, 1-6.

1. Confirmed by other sources: Confirmed by other independent sources; logical in itself; Consistent with other information on the subject
2. Probably True: Not confirmed; logical in itself; consistent with other information on the subject
3. Possibly True: Not confirmed; reasonably logical in itself; agrees with some other information on the subject
4. Doubtful: Not confirmed; possible but not logical; no other information on the subject
5. Improbable: Not confirmed; not logical in itself; contradicted by other information on the subject
6. Truth cannot be judged: No basis exists for evaluating the validity of the information

Analysis of Competing Hypotheses

Analysis of competing hypotheses[1] (ACH) is a process whereby you identify a set of hypotheses, systematically evaluate data that is consistent and inconsistent with each hypothesis, and reject the hypotheses that contain too much inconsistent data.

ACH is a tool to aid judgment on important issues which require careful weighing of alternative explanations or conclusions. It helps an analyst to overcome, or at least minimize, some of the cognitive limitations that make intelligence analysis so difficult.

ACH is an eight-step procedure which is an effective, proven process to help analysts avoid common pitfalls. It is particularly appropriate for complex issues when analysts want to leave an audit trail to demonstrate what they considered and how they arrived at their judgment.

ANALYSIS OF COMPETING HYPOTHESES

1. **HYPOTHESIS**

2. **EVIDENCE**

3. **DIAGNOSTICS**

4. **REFINEMENT**

5. **INCONSISTENCY**

6. **SENSITIVITY**

7. **CONCLUSIONS AND EVALUATION**

Security Risk Management Aide-Memoire

EVIDENCE	Hackers are stealing commercial information	Insiders are selling commercial information	Listening devices have been placed in our offices
Our quotes are consistently and narrowly beaten on price	C	C	C
Many of our exact phrases in competitor bids	C	C	I
Leaked information is from all departments	C	I	I
Network security is unsophisticated	C	I	I
Network traffic heightened prior to major bids	C	I	I

C = Consistent   I = Inconsistent

Criticality Assessment

There are many ways to assess criticality. This diagram is one example and is a part of the larger integrated diagram in PART D: MODELS AND FRAMEWORKS: SRMBOK Methodology.

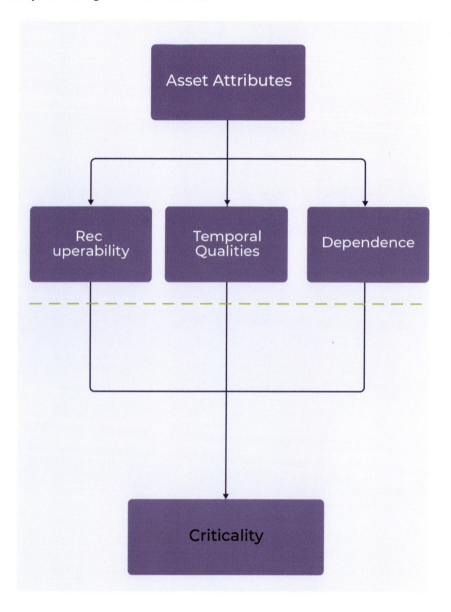

Vulnerability Analysis

Vulnerability Analysis

A vulnerability assessment is the process of identifying, quantifying, and prioritizing (or ranking) the vulnerabilities in a system. Examples of systems for which vulnerability assessments are performed include, but are not limited to, information technology systems, energy supply systems, water supply systems, transportation systems, and communication systems.

Vulnerability analysis is related to Business Impact Analysis (BIA) but takes a particular focus, that of identifying specific weaknesses.

The diagram below is a part of the SRMBOK Methodology in PART D: MODELS AND FRAMEWORKS.

Security Risk Management Aide-Memoire

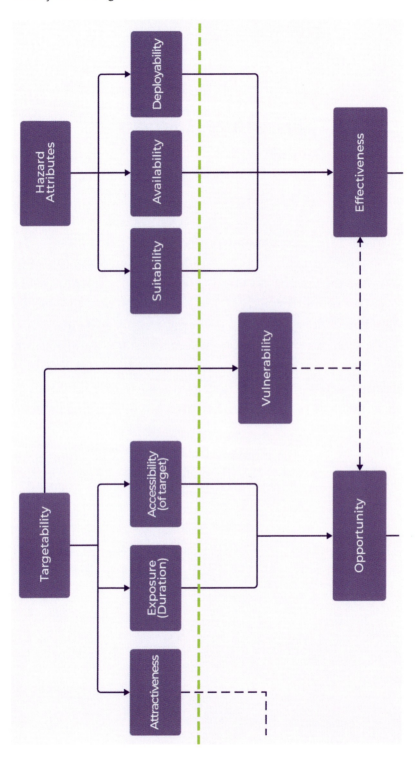

PART C: ADDITIONAL TOOLS

* * *

CARVER[1] is an example of a vulnerability analysis too and stands for:
1. Criticality - a measure of the public health and economic impacts of an attack
2. Accessibility - the ability to physically access and egress from a target
3. Recuperability - the ability of system to recover from an attack
4. Vulnerability - the ease of accomplishing an attack
5. Effect - the consequences or amount of direct loss from an attack as measured by loss in production
6. Recognizability - ease of identifying a target

OCTAVE[2] can also be useful in determining vulnerability and stands for: **Operationally Critical Threat, Asset, and Vulnerability Evaluation.**

Risk Analysis

Inputs to aid risk analysis can include the elements listed below. Note: The grouping (input, process, output, feedback) is purely thematic, designed to link with standard management systems. It should not be taken to imply that these are the only or best way to consider risk analysis.

Inputs
- Nature and characteristics of risks
- Level and priority of risks
- Uncertainties, assumptions, & unknowns
- Sources, threats, hazards
- Immediate and root causes
- Time and frequency related factors
- Availability/reliability of information and costs/resources involved in attaining additional information

Processes
- Likelihood/probability
- Events, scenarios, and vulnerabilities
- Controls and effectiveness of controls

Outputs
- Consequences (nature & magnitude)
- Outputs from a range of techniques

Feedback
- Complexity/connectivity of events
- Volatility (events, threats, etc)
- Limitations of the analysis techniques

Inherent Risk

Risk Estimation

Risk is an abstract concept and humans are notoriously bad at predicting it.[1] A 1% chance of an event occurring does not mean that it won't happen. Even subject matter experts are notoriously poor at calculating risks.[2] Unfortunately, two of the common methods (WAGNER and BOGSAT methods - explained in the graphic below) are the least reliable.

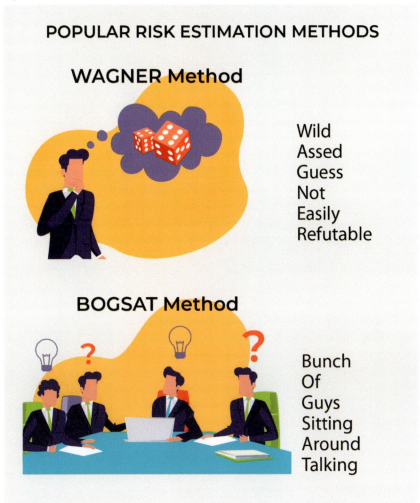

More comprehensive methods of risk identification and

estimation, require additional information, which usually comes at a greater cost. There are however, many relatively low cost ways to improve risk estimation. There is compelling research to indicate that risk matrices can often produce an inferior result to more quantitative methods.[3]

FORMAL RISK ESTIMATION METHODS

Below is some general guidance to help improve the accuracy of estimates:

- Try to understand from the start, what you do and do

not know and to what level of certainty/uncertainty.

- Always seek and use the best available data, no matter how limited it may be. Where possible use annotated data, peer-reviewed research, quantitative data and statistical analysis to assess risk. Where this is not possible, document a) the nature and source of available information, b) the level of uncertainty, and c) any additional information that would be helpful and the cost of attaining it.

- Where comprehensive data is not available, it will still be useful to state whatever is reasonably known. For example: "We have 90% confidence that a server outage due to system breach will take at least 30 minutes to resolve but not more than 24 hours. Experience indicates that it is unlikely (5%) that we can bring it back online in under 30 minutes, and equally unlikely (5%) that it will take longer than 24 hours."

- Use structured, defensible arguments such as causality diagrams, Analysis of Competing Hypotheses, Root Cause Analysis, 8 Step Process, Expected Monetary Value, and some of the frameworks from the following pages.

- Consider what additional data is required, and factor in the time/cost of acquiring it.

- Break your estimates down to the right level of granularity - the more specific or granular the estimates, the more likely they are to be accurate.

- Use Subject Matter Experts (SMEs) who are

'calibrated'. Calibrated probability assessments are subjective probabilities assigned by individuals who have been trained to assess probabilities in a way that historically represents their uncertainty. By practicing with a series of trivia questions, it is possible for subjects to fine-tune their ability to assess probabilities.

- Avoid making a point estimate. Instead develop a *range* of possible outcomes. Eg: a 90% confidence that Attack 'A' if successful, will cost between $1 million and $8 million. This at least clarifies the range of uncertainty.

- Consider using Monte Carlo Simulation for more complex analysis.

- Use causation diagrams such as Root Cause Analysis or Ishikawa Diagrams.

- Where possible, calculate an Expected Monetary Value.

Risk Matrices

Risk matrices are commonly used in security and other risk management practices. There are a number of issues with risk matrices and overall, I would discourage their use. That is not to say that they don't have a place but caution is advised in using them. If you have to use a risk matrix due for example, to corporate policy, the following advice may help.

Limitations of Risk Matrices

Some of the problems with risk matrices are that they can:
- Assign identical ratings to quantitatively different risks.
- Lead to errors in risk prioritization, as calculation of consequences cannot be made objectively for uncertain outcomes.
- Rely on subject matter expert judgements, resulting in wide variations in risk ratings, as different users assess differing likelihood and consequence ratings
- Unless explicitly stated, lead to assumptions regarding timeframes and frequencies of activities or events
- Oversimplify the volatility of a risk, as some risks are relatively static over time while others can change rapidly
- Lead assessors to overlook causation and downstream consequences

For an overview of some of the limitations of risk matrices, see "What's Wrong With Risk Matrices".[1]

Avoid If Possible

If using risk matrices, it's best to avoid:
- Using simple (eg: 2x2) risk matrices as a risk calculation tool. They have some uses for initial discussion or prioritization (See: Stroud Matrix) but are unable to provide accurate prioritization of risks.

- Plotting risks as a single point value of likelihood and consequence. All risks are likely to have a range of consequences and should be plotted accordingly. See: Bubble Charts for an example.
- Risk matrices where risks which have the same semi-quantitative ranking (ordinal or priority ranking) have differing quantitative values. For example, on a 5x5 matrix, if risk 'A' has a likelihood of 2 and consequence of 4 it will have a priority ranking of 6. If a likelihood of 2 is 20% and consequence of 4 is $10 million the Expected Monetary Value (EMV) will be $2 million. Similarly risk 'B' with likelihood of 4 (80%) and consequence of 2 ($1 million) will also rank as a 6 but have an EMV of $800,000. Although both have a rating of 6, the EMVs of $800,000 and $2,000,000 are substantially different.

When Using Risk Matrices

If you do wish to, or are required to use risk matrices, some of the best ways to use them include:
- Express ratings as a probability distribution across several squares.
- Use quantitative measures such as 0.0 to 1.0 for probability, and $0 to $X for consequence, where $X is the equity of the organization (or the quantity of cash or other items which would ensure the total demise of the organization if it eventuated).
- As a framework for discussion.
- Providing calibration training to users beforehand.
- Using explicit likelihood and consequence descriptors which are as quantitative as possible; and then check and confirm at each stage that the team share the same understanding of the risks and the relevant descriptors.
- Use only risk statements which have been clearly defined. See: Risk Identification and Risk Statements.

- Using a matrix with more granularity (eg: a 10x10 matrix) to limit any tendency to cluster risks on a single setting.
- Brainstorming risk events based on concepts of likelihood, for example, by considering what are the most likely and unlikely risk events.
- Brainstorming risk events based on consequences, by considering the nature and relative significance of consequences in comparison to each other, prioritizing the consequences, and then moving 'upstream' to consider the potential sources and causes of such events.
- Contrasting and discussing risks in a comparative fashion, e.g. Is the organization's risk from attack by an external hacker attack greater or lesser than the risk from a insider threat? If so, by how much and why? What are the causes and effects of each?
- As a framework for communicating comparative risk ratings and quality of controls. For an example of how to use risk matrices as a communication tool see Communication and "What's Right With Risk Matrices[2]".

Opportunities

Note: the traditional view of risk is negative, representing loss and adverse consequences and the following risk matrix examples describe only negative consequences. ISO31000 includes the possibility of positive risk or opportunity associated with uncertainties that could have a beneficial effect on achieving objectives.[3] It is equally practical to construct positive risk matrices, or matrices which show both positive and negative consequences. See SRMBOK, Figure 6.11 for an example.

Likelihood and Consequence Tables

There is no single correct way to express likelihood or consequence tables. Each organization needs to consider their context and develop specific tables or metrics to suit their situation.

With that caveat, the following pages offer two examples of how such tables might be established. Your organization may choose to use only one, or perhaps various ways to group likelihood and consequence.

In the following examples, there are four categories for Likelihood and six categories for Consequences. Use the minimum number necessary to achieve your goal.

Guidance note: when using such tables choose
1. The most statistically likely, or at least most credible likelihood for an event occurring
2. The range of potential consequences which you are 90% confident that the consequences will fall between, e.g. in the range of 3 to 5 (Moderate to Significant). The more precise the better but if you do not have solid evidence, this approach will at least allow you to express your level of uncertainty. This will help identify the level and type of information required in order to improve your predictions.

Likelihood Tables

The following is one example of how likelihood tables can be structured.

Qualitative Likelihood	Historical Occurrences	Natural Frequencies	Probability
Is expected to occur in most circumstances	Has occurred on an regular basis in the organization during the timeframe being considered or circumstances are in train that will cause it to happen	Is likely, or has been known to occur 90 times every 100 timeframes	0.90 (0.80-0.99)
Will probably occur in most circumstances	Has occurred in the organization within 3 multiples of the timeframe being considered.	Is likely, or has been known to occur roughly 70 times in 100	0.70 (0.61-0.80)
Might occur at some time	Has occurred previously in the history of the organization and/or in other similar organizations or circumstances	Is likely, or has been known to occur approximately 50 out of 100 times	0.50 (0.41-0.60)
Could occur at some time	Has never occurred in this organizaion but has occurred infrequently in other similar organizations	Is likely, or has been known to occur less than 1 in 10,000 times	0.30 (0.21-0.40)
Can only occur in exceptional circumstances	Is possible but has not occurred to date in this or any similar organizations	Is likely, or has been known to occur less than once in 100 timeframes	0.10 (0.01-0.20)

Consequence Tables

Consequence tables need to be customized for each specific organization or context. The following is just one example.

Security Risk Management Aide-Memoire

PEOPLE	Minor injury or first aid treatment	Injury requiring treatment by medical practitioner and/or lost time from workplace.	Major injury / hospitalization	Single death and/or multiple major injuries	Multiple deaths
INFORMATION	Compromise of information otherwise available in the public domain.	Minor compromise of information sensitive to internal or sub-unit interests.	Compromise of information sensitive to the organizations operations.	Compromise of information sensitive to organizational interests.	Compromise of information with significant ongoing impact.
PROPERTY	Minor damage or vandalism to asset.	Minor damage or loss of <5% of total assets	Damage or loss of <20% of total assets	Extensive damage or loss of ~50% of total assets	Destruction or complete loss of >50% of assets
ECOMONIC	1% of budget or revenue (organizational, division or project budget as relevant)	10-20% of budget	40-60% of budget or revenue	60-80% of budget or revenue	>80% of project or organizational budget or revenue
REPUTATION	Local mention only. Quickly forgotten.	Scrutiny by Executive, internal committees or internal audit to prevent escalation. Short term local media concern. Some impact on local level activities	Persistent national concern. Scrutiny required by external agencies. Long term 'brand' impact.	Persistent intense national public, political and media scrutiny.	International concern, Governmental Inquiry or sustained adverse national/international media. 'Brand' significantly affects organizational abilities.
CAPABILITY	Minor skills impact. Minimal impact on non-core operations. The impact can be dealt with by routine operations.	Some impact on organizational capability in terms of delays, systems quality but able to be dealt with at operational level	Impact on the organization resulting in reduced performance such that targets are not met. Organizations existence is not threatened, but could be subject to significant review.	Breakdown of key activities leading to reduction in performance (eg. service delays, revenue loss, client dissatisfaction, legislative breaches).	Protracted unavailability of critical skills/people. Critical failure(s) preventing core activities from being performed. Survival of the project/activity/organization is threatened.

Risk Analysis

Example 5x5 Risk Matrix

The examples below are purely indicative of what various risk matrices might look like.

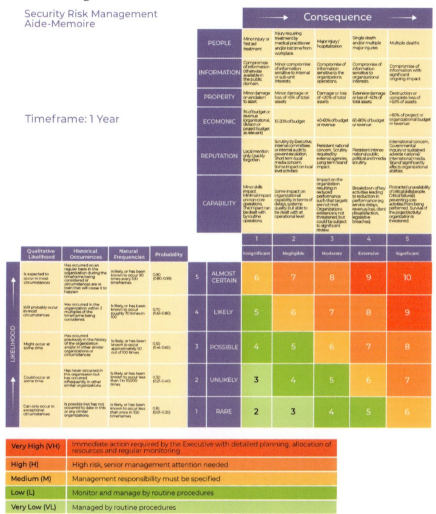

You can find enlarged versions of the metrics in the section on Likelihood And Consequence Tables.

Example 11x11 Risk Matrix

The following matrix shows an example of how three different risks (A, B, C) might be plotted on a matrix in a way which reflects the uncertainty of those risks.

For example, Risk C has been assessed as having a roughly 10% likelihood of eventuating. The probability distribution as shown on the matrix might have been created based on historical data, expert judgement, or a Monte Carlo Simulation. The main point however is that the illustration shows that a risk with 10% likelihood of eventuating is considered most likely to generate losses which are equivalent to 40% to 50% of organizational equity. But it also shows that there is a slight chance that this risk might also create a 95% loss event.

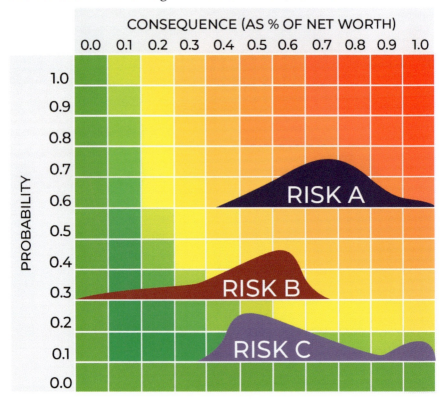

Using the x-axis to show potential consequences as a

percentage of organizational equity is one way to express as percentages of total loss. In this instance, it's been assumed that losing 100% of more of total equity would be an existential threat to the organization. Risks which generate losses greater than 100% of equity have equal 'consequence' ranking to 100% risks. This is because, to the organization, a 500% loss event has no greater consequence than the bankruptcy which would result from a 100% or 125%, etc loss event.

The x-axis in this example, could be replaced by actual dollar amounts, or equally by any risk considered as being existential. This might be multiple deaths, massive damage to reputation, etc.

Stroud Matrix

The objective of this tool is to aid discussion and provide an initial categorization of risks into four groups:

- **BUSINESS AS USUAL** (BAU): Risks that are unlikely to occur and will probably have only minor consequences if they do. Examples include fraud, common burglary, vandalism, and shoplifting. Some analysis and ongoing monitoring might be appropriate but these risks are typically best managed by standard procedures.
- **ROUTINE**: Risks that are likely to occur but if managed correctly will rarely result in catastrophic consequences. Examples include phishing attacks, network penetration attempts, minor theft, etc. Usually managed by standard operating procedures.
- **SWANS**: Risks that are unlikely but are likely to have major consequences if they eventuate. 'Black Swans'[1] refer to unidentified risks while 'White Swans' include foreseeable but rare risks. A terrorist attack using an improvised explosive device would be and example of a White Swan, 9/11 was a Black Swan. Monitoring and detailed analysis is likely to be appropriate for these risks.
- **DANGER ZONE**: Risks that are both likely to occur and likely to have major consequences. Depending on the organization, examples might include international operations in high risk environments, industrial espionage, or privacy breaches. These require detailed analysis and specific resources, and should be the priority for senior management and risk analysts.

* * *

Risk Analysis

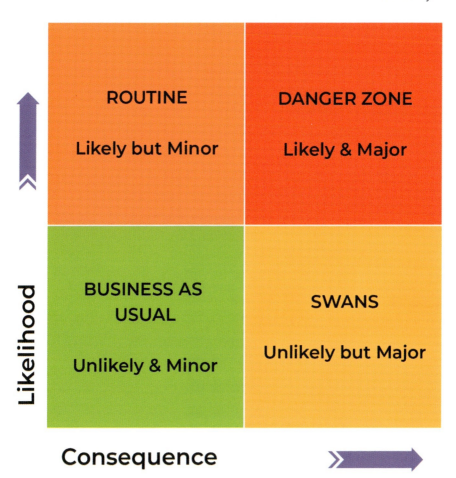

As to why it's called Stroud Matrix? No particular reason but it needed a name and it was created in the town of Stroud in the Cotswolds in the UK.

Probability of an Event

One of the challenges with Security Risk Assessment is the analysis of rare but catastrophic events. Events for which we often lack solid data and, by definition, are abstract and unlikely, but with consequences so dire that we cannot ignore them. And sadly, they are more common than we might expect.

Catastrophic attacks with a tiny likelihood of occurring in any given year are almost certain to happen over a longer horizon. In the words of Chuck Palahniuk in the novel, Fight Club, "On a long enough time line, the survival rate for everyone drops to zero."

Consider the maths of calculating the probability of an event such as the metaphorical one-in-one-hundred year storm, or a notional Black Swan event such as 9/11.

a. If we call P the probability of attack 'A' happening in any given year, we can express this as: $P(A) = 1\% = 0.01$

b. The chance of not having a P(A) event this year, denoted as P(A') and pronounced P of A-prime, is therefore 1 - P(A), or 99% (1 - 0.01 = 0.99)

c. The likelihood of having no 'A' for 2 years = $P(A') * P(A') = P(A')^2 = 0.99*0.99 = 0.9801$

d. P(A' for X years) = $P(A')^X$. Therefore P(no attack of type A for 30 years) = $P(A')^{30} = 0.99^{30} = 0.7397$

This means that over a thirty-year period, the probability of not having an attack of type A is approximately 74 percent. By inference, the probability of one attack of type A in the next 30 years is more than one in four (26%).

Now consider four other rare, but catastrophic attacks, each with no correlation to each other. They could be anything but let's say for example: cyberattack, bombing, active shooter, and information breach. At the risk of over-simplifying independent versus dependent probability, if the chance of any individual event happening in the next 30 years is 26%, the likelihood of any one happening in the same period is 100%.

When we grow the list of rare events, the likelihood of an attack happening with near certainty goes from once in 100 years, to one in 30 years, to 20 years, to 10 years, etc. In other words, the next rare, but extreme attack may be just about to happen.

Three Point Estimation

Three point estimation is one way to calculate a realistic estimation using a best case estimate, worst case estimate and most likely case estimate. There are different ways of using these numbers, depending on how you want to weight the result, but a simple way to use the data is to use the formula

(Best + Worst + Most likely) / 3 = Expected estimate

As an example, after discussing with your team, you estimate the cost of an event as follows:

- Best – $3,000
- Worst – $9,000
- Most likely – $5,000

    (Best + Worst + Most likely) / 3 = Expected estimate
    (3,000 + 9,000 + 5,000) / 3 = $5,700

    You might also apply probabilities to estimates. Eg:

- Best case might be assessed as having a probability of 20% (0.2 or P20),
- Worst as 20% likely (P20), and
- Most Likely as being 60% likely (P60).

    In such as case you might calculate the estimated cost of an attack as being:

    ($3,000 * 0.2) + ($9,000 * 0.2) + ($5,000 * 0.6) = $5,400

    Note: In the above example the probabilities add up to 100%

Expected Monetary Value

While it is difficult to precisely quantify all loss events, even after they occur (e.g. the event's impact on your brand), many risks can be reasonably quantified. One approach is know as Expected Monetary Value (EMV) or Expected Loss (EL).

> A) 30% chance of $1,000,000 loss ($300,000)
> B) 20% chance of $500,000 loss ($100,000)
> C) 50% chance of $100,000 loss ($50,000)

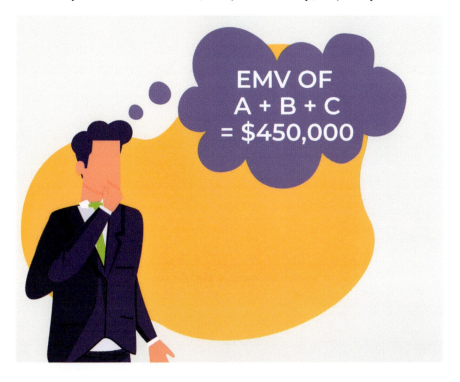

This involves calculating a range of potential likelihoods and consequences. Imagine if someone challenges you to you "toss this coin and I will give you $10,000 if it comes up heads and $20,000 if it comes up tails". It's a 50/50 bet so 0.5 probability for each outcome and your EMV for this wonderful arrangement would be $15,000. The calculation is:

(50% * $10,000) + (50% * $20,000)

= $5,000 + $10,000

= $15,000.

You might assess that your supermarket has an 80% likelihood of losing $200,000 from shoplifters this year and a 20% chance of keeping that loss down to $100,000

(0.80 * $200,000) + (0.20 * $100,000) = $160,000 + $20,000 = Expected Loss (EL) of $180,000

Therefore any security measures which are 100% effective (hypothetically) and cost less than $180,000 per year are likely to be worthwhile.

If CCTV will reduce your expected losses by 50% (to $90,000) but will cost $60,000 per year, it has an EMV benefit of $40,000 per year.

- Existing situation = $180,000 EL
- Upgrade = $60,000 p.a. for CCTV costs + $90,000 p.a. in losses due to shoplifting = $150,000 per year; $30,000 lower than current situation. An EMV of $30,000 improvement compared to no CCTV.

P90, P50, P10

Another approach to using multiple point estimation involves using probabilities which do not add up to 100%. We might for example, say that an arson attack on your office is 90% likely (Probability = 90% or 'P90') to be put out quickly by the state of the art fire suppression system with a loss of less than $100,000.

There might, hypothetically, be a 50% chance (P50) that the fire could cause $2 million damage, but it would be very unlikely (P10) to cause a catastrophic loss with costs of $20 million. This would be expressed as "If there is an arson attack" the likely consequences are:

- P90 - $100,000
- P50 - $2,000,000
- P10 - $20,000,000

This system isn't designed to be mathematically accurate but is useful for discussing the likelihood of various consequences with stakeholders, to establish range estimates. It might also be expressed in terms of 'almost certain', 'possible', and 'very unlikely'. You might for example, based on past years, consider your likely expected loss (EL) for annual theft as being:

P90 (almost certain) to lose $50,000 = 0.90 * $50,000 = $45,000 EL

P50 (credible scenario) a loss of $150,000 = 0.50 * $150,000 = $75,000 EL

P10 (worst case but unlikely) loss of $1,000,000 = 0.10 * $1,000,000 = $100,000 EL

With discussion, you might expand this to:

EXPECTED LOSS	PROBABILITY
$10,000	99%
$20,000	95%
$45,000	**90%**
$50,000	80%
$60,000	70%
$65,000	60%
$75,000	**50%**
$80,000	40%
$85,000	30%
$90,000	20%
$100,000	**10%**
$200,000	5%
$400,000	1%

Plotted on a chart, you can see the range of expected likely outcomes. If there is a successful arson attack, the chance of a loss in excess of $200,000 is close to zero.

Risk Analysis

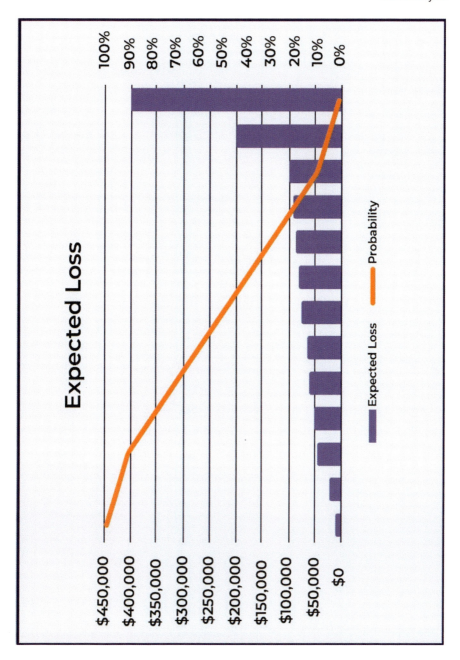

Modeling Risk Expectancy

By spreading the outcomes such that the total percentage is 100% you can effectively say, this is the total range of possible outcomes, and produce an EMV.

In this case it is $61,750. From the chart, you can also see the most likely range of losses, and the potential outliers for the worst case.

The following example and chart is for just one hypothetical risk which considers, for example, the expected costs (based on historical data, other evidence or expert judgement) of loss due to shoplifting over the coming 12 months.

If you did this for a range of other risks, then calculated the aggregated scores for key risks in this fashion, a probability curve for expected loss can be plotted. This at least provides a view of the potential range of consequences, including extreme outliers, and provides insight for management as to the level of uncertainty.

Douglass Hubbard and Richard Seiersen explain all this and much more in great detail in their book, How to Measure Anything in Cybersecurity Risk[1].

Ultimately the purpose is to inform decision making and help determine which risks require priority treatment and to what extent.

EL	PROB.	EMV
$10,000	4%	$400
$20,000	10%	$2,000
$45,000	**25%**	$11,250
$50,000	12%	$6,000
$60,000	11%	$6,600
$65,000	9%	$5,850
$75,000	**8%**	$6,000
$80,000	6%	$4,800
$85,000	5%	$4,250
$90,000	4%	$3,600
$100,000	**3%**	$3,000
$200,000	2%	$4,000
$400,000	1%	$4,000
	100%	**$61,750**

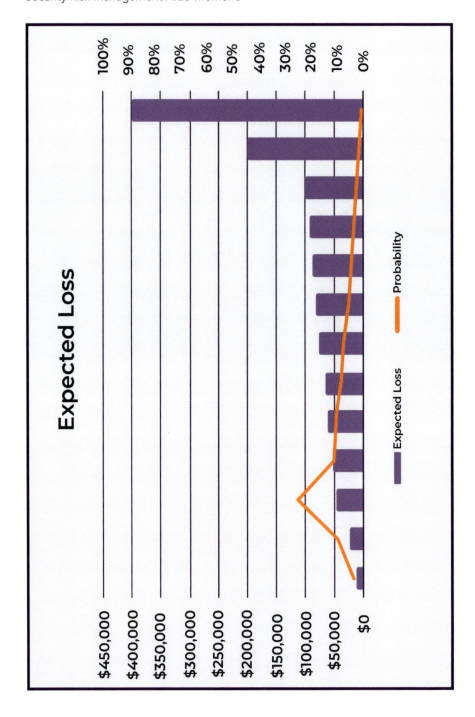

Risk Evaluation

To evaluate risks, refer to the sections of this book on:
- Threat Tolerance
- Risk Tolerance
- Criteria
- Likelihood And Consequence Tables
- Writing A Risk Statement

Risk Treatments

The Nature of Risk Treatments

Here are several levels of expenditure to consider when implementing treatments:
- Sunk costs – funds that have already been irrevocably committed.
- Compliance Costs – costs of doing business (legally) or essentially, the 'license to operate'.
- Base (or Prudent) Costs – basic costs to provide essential basic risk management.
- Best Practice – investments that achieve an appropriate return on investment (ROI) to reduce risk to As Low as Reasonably Practicable (ALARP - Ref: PART A: CORE CONCEPTS)
- Discretionary – items which may or may not achieve a required ROI but are likely to reduce risk even further.

Cost Effectiveness

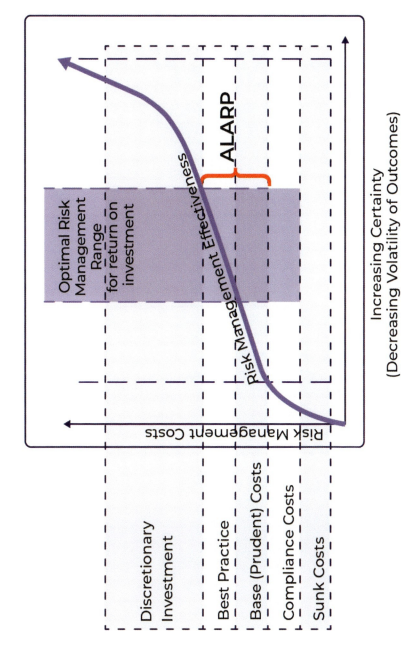

Selecting Risk Treatments

ISO31000 suggests applying one or more of the following approaches to treating risks:
- Avoiding the risk by deciding not to start or continue with the activity that gives rise to the risk
- Removing the risk source
- Changing the likelihood
- Changing the consequences
- Sharing the risk (e.g. through contracts, buying insurance)
- Retaining the risk by informed decision
- Taking or increasing the risk in order to pursue an opportunity

Some treatments will be more effective than others. Some will focus on likelihood and others on consequence management. Any one risk treatment will usually also address other risks, incidentally or directly. See also DDDRR, Hierarchy of Controls, Risk Tolerance, and Criteria.

Risk Treatments

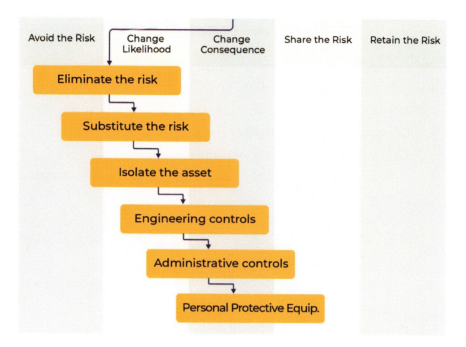

Writing Risk Treatments - 4As

Risk treatments and recommendations can benefit from the 4A model. It can also be used to analyze the quality of existing security plans or recommendations.

- Appropriate: Addresses the root cause.
- Actionable: Specific timeframes, actions, resources, and accountable personnel to implement the treatment/recommendation.
- Achievable: Criteria, individual judgement, or milestone by which the recommendation will be considered complete.
- Agreed: Relevant personnel who were consulted and support this.

EXAMPLE: *After consultation with the Head of HR and Chief Security Officer (e.g. AGREED), the team recommend that external contractors selected by the CSO will update all servers to the current software version (e.g. ACHIEVABLE) within 7 days (e.g. ACTIONABLE), and that the additional full-time staff be recruited by HR (e.g. APPROPRIATE) to commence within 30 days.*

Eight Step Process For Selecting Risk Treatments

The following process can help identify treatments for complex risks. It can be used for a facilitated brainstorming workshop, as report headings, and stakeholder engagement.

1. What is the risk? The risk statement must be comprehensive, leaving no room for error about what is really meant.
2. Why is it a risk? What are the root causes and vulnerabilities? How will it impact objectives?
3. What is/are the source/s of the risk? What are the hazards? Who or what are likely threat actors and what acts are they committing?
4. What are the possible risk treatments? All ideas should be listed in the initial brainstorm no matter how impractical or difficult to implement.
5. What is the best treatment (or treatments)?
6. Why is this the best treatment/s? Does it directly address the root cause of the risk stated in question one? Is it the best solution in terms of the hierarchy of controls? Does it reduce the risk to ALARP?
7. What action(s) must be taken to implement it? Who will be responsible? What resources will be required? How will it be measured as being completed successfully? When must/should it be completed by?
8. What have we not thought of? Search for possible flaws in your proposed treatment, which could be exposed by a question from stakeholders. Any question the stakeholders can think of, you can think of. Develop a Q&A list of potential issues and responses.

Designing Treatment Plans

1. Define the Risk
   - Source
   - Event
   - Resources affected
   - Consequences
   - Likelihood
2. Brainstorm
   - List options
   - Risk criteria
   - Tolerance for risk
   - Objectives of the risk treatments
3. Prioritize
   - Hierarchy of Controls (ESIEAP) - Ref: PART A: CORE CONCEPTS, Hierarchy of Controls
4. Define
   - 4As - Ref: Writing Risk Treatments (4As)
5. Consider
   - Downstream impacts
   - Unintended consequences
   - New risks introduced

6. Implementation
    - Who:
        - Responsible
        - Accountable
    - When:
        - Start date
        - Finish date
        - Milestones
    - What:
        - Work Breakdown Structure
        - Tasks
        - Sequencing
    - How:
        - Elements
        - Activities
        - Processes
        - Systems
    - Resources:
        - Money
        - People
        - Materials

Treatment Plans

The following headings may be suitable for many treatment registers.

- Serial (Treatment ID)
- Treatment
- Description
- Risks Treated (Risk IDs)
- Initial Cost
- Ongoing/Recurrent Cost
- Priority
- Cost Implications For Other Activities
- Acceptance (Yes/No)
- Actionee (The recipient of an action item; the person assigned responsibility for a specific task or issue.)
- Due Date

Documenting Complex Treatments

The following elements provide an example of a high level overview of complex risk treatments. Each risk treatment in the Treatment Register might for example, require a single page outlining the following elements. That single page, might constitute an overview of a multi-million dollar, multi-year project.

- **Description:** high level description of the treatment
- **Actions:** three to seven steps required to implement
- **Achieved when:** criteria or person which will determine completion
- **Risks Treated:** list of risks or risk identifiers which are addressed by this treatment
- Agreed by: persons or stakeholder groups consulted
- **Scope:** types of risks, geography, groups, etc.
- **Schedule:** timeframe for implementation or cycle (e.g. annual review)
- **Resources:** money, personnel, equipment required
- **Quality:** standards or criteria for implementation
- **Lead Agent:** person responsible
- **Implementation Parameters:** references to documentation, processes (e.g. PRINCE2), etc.
- **Rationale and Application:** links to other projects and rationale for choosing this treatment over others
- **Hierarchy of Controls:** risk approach (engineering, administrative, etc. see: Hierarchy of Controls)
- **Bow-Tie:** focus (likelihood or consequence management or both)

Risk Communication

Communication and consultation is an iterative, two (or more) way process, which applies at all stages of risk management. Miscommunication can also be a source of risk and a barrier to reacting to it.

Bubble Charts

The following is an example of three risks plotted on an X-Y chart using Likelihood and Consequence. Note that the risks are not indicated as points but rather as regions to indicate the level of uncertainty regarding likelihood and consequence.

For simplicity only estimated probability and financial impacts (rather than reputation, etc.) have been used but the same could apply to any likelihood and consequence measures.

The relative ranking, location, and size however, provides insights as to priorities and whether to focus on likelihood management or consequence management, or both.

In the following example, CyberAttack is certain, however the range of possible costs is unknown. Similarly the cost of loss of capability is relatively low but the likelihood is less clearly understood.

Security Risk Management Aide-Memoire

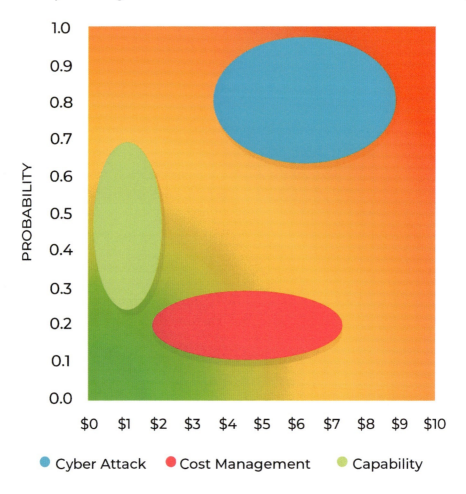

Visual Risk Models For Communication

The following tools can be useful for communicating risk visually:
- Swiss-Cheese
- Hierarchy of Controls
- Ishikawa Diagrams
- Root Cause Analysis
- Risk Matrices
- Bubble Charts

Security Briefings

The five paragraph order technique, also known as SMEAC, is a technique used by many military agencies to deliver a team briefing in a consistent format.

SITUATION
Background, scope, location, people, related work, etc

MISSION
Succinct, precise, and unambiguous expression of intention and objectives.

EXECUTION
Who does what, when, and how.

ADMIN & LOG
Coordination, equipment, logistics, paperwork and other details.

COMMAND & COMMS
Communication protocols, leadership structures, and responsibilities.

Situation

This is the context of the task and provides a snapshot or background to the subsequent instructions.

- Name of the task
- Scope, geography, context, criteria
- Objectives
- Any prior related work
- Future use of the outcomes from this task
- Other activities that might be affected by this assignment
- Relevant information, files, reference documents, emails or discussions
- Other teams that will or may need to be involved

Mission

The mission is the intent of the task. The mission statement is a short, clear and concise statement of what you want to achieve. The mission statement is a precise expression of the objective. In a military setting it is repeated twice for emphasis.

e.g. *"The mission is to research and establish the nature and frequency of cyberattacks on similar organizations in the past two years"*.

Execution

Execution is the "how" part of the plan – how you are going to achieve your mission.

- Detail the steps required, including Who, What, Where, When, Why and How.
- What are you going to do? Why? When? Where? Who is involved? How?
- The execution part of the process is usually the longest and should provide sufficient information to allow the team to go and do the job.
- Often broken up into 2 to 5 phases (steps).

Administration and Logistics

The resources and people involved, logistics, supply chain,

and how resources are to be coordinated, documentation to be required, responsibilities for equipment, etc.

Command and Communications

Who is in charge, who does each person report to.

Methods, timing, and frequency of communication both within the team and to/from external parties.

Recording Observations

When conducting a security risk assessment, it is important to document some of the key findings as evidence to support the risk register and proposed treatments.

Some of the findings may not be significant enough to warrant a risk statement or treatment, yet may still be worth noting as a finding and perhaps including a recommendation to address the issue.

Findings

During the course of security risk assessments, you may discover additional material worthy of comment. You might, for example, find a vulnerability in terms of a router being incorrectly configured. This in itself isn't a risk *per se*, but needs to be recorded. Equally an electronic access control system which gives everyone 24-hour access and doesn't use time or zone controls is a weakness even if it isn't specifically a risk.

The 4C model is helpful for recording audit findings or observations during a security risk assessment. It can also be used to analyze the quality of existing report findings.

- Condition. What condition was observed?
- Criteria. What should have been observed? What audit or best practice criteria were relevant?
- Cause. What are the immediate and underlying root causes of the condition?
- Consequence. What is the actual or potential impact on

objectives or resources/assets?

EXAMPLE: *The review noted that 6 out of 10 servers are not running the current software version (CONDITION) despite the organizational security plan which mandated that servers be updated within 7 days of stable software upgrades (CRITERIA). Known vulnerabilities in the old software versions may enable third-parties to access commercially sensitive data (CONSEQUENCE). The (immediate) cause is lack of resources in the security team due to delays in recruiting the additional three personnel (root CAUSE) funded in the security plan.*

Recommendations

Recommendations should:
- Address the cause and diminish the effect for the matter noted
- Stand alone (i.e. Still make sense when read in isolation)
- Start with an action word (eg: "Replace..." not "Consider replacing...")
- Be doable
- Add value

Note: Keep the number of recommendations to minimum – unnecessary recommendations damage credibility and dilute impact.

Recommendations should also be SMART:
- Specific
- Measurable
- Actionable
- Realistic
- Timebound

Assessing the Quality of SRM

One element that is often missing or inadequate is how to ensure, and to assess the effectiveness of security risk management and security assessments.

Indicators

The following are examples of some indicators which should be evident in a security risk assessment or management system.
- Accountability - risk acceptance. The individual who accepted the risk is clearly identified.
- Accountability - risk treatment. The individual who is responsible for treating the risk is clearly identified. Ref: Documenting Complex Treatments
- Existing controls. Explicitly identified and linked to risks. Ref: 11. Controls
- Scope, Context, and Criteria are clearly identified. Ref: 7. Scope, Context, Criteria
- Consequences and likelihood are assessed and supporting evidence is referenced. Ref: 16. Risk Analysis
- Methodology of risk and threat assessments are documented, use (or adapt) a robust and recognized framework or methodology. Ref: References
- Threat and risk assessments follow and comply with the identified methodology. Eg: 5. SRMBOK Methodology, 2. ISO31000 Risk Management Standard

- Human Factors are considered and documented. Ref: A6. Human Factors(HFACS)
- Risk assessment tools are correctly applied and minimize biases or subjectivity as much as possible. Ref: 16. Risk Analysis
- Risk assessment tools are appropriate for the scale of the activity. See: A1. The Right Tool For Each Job.
- Risk statements meet the criteria outlined in '14. Risk Statements'. Ref: Writing a Risk Statement
- Risk Treatments are explicitly linked to risks and address root cause(s). Ref: A11. Root Cause Analysis.

10 Point Scale: Guidance For Assessment Of SRM/ A Quality Indicators

The following 10-point scale is designed to provide guidance when assessing the quality of security risk assessments and management systems.

1. No intention to implement the requirements of the indicator.
2. Some awareness and intention to implement. May be limited or inadequate action to implement at this stage.
3. Early progress toward implementation. Evidence of management commitment of resources to the requirements of the indicator.
4. Preparation for consistent implementation is well under way. Early drafts of documents supporting the indicator may be available.
5. Basic requirements of the indicator are almost in place. Documents may be in draft form. Planning may have occurred but plans are not fully implemented. Implementation of the basic requirements of the indicator is imminent.
6. Satisfies minimum requirements of the indicator. Basic documentation can be produced if specified in the indicator. System may be relatively new but there is evidence that requirements are applied within the organisation. Compliance with minimum standards and/or relevant legislation.
7. Basic documentation supports the requirements of the indicator even though it may not be specified in the indicator itself. Continuous improvement processes developing and regularly demonstrated in documentary form. Monitoring procedures in place as part of continuous improvement.
8. Requirements of the indicator have been in place long

enough to allow evaluation and review. Maintaining more than the minimum requirements, but room for improvement. Strong supporting documentation. Ongoing continuous improvement.

9. Sustained performance in parts of the organisation where the requirements of the indicator apply. Some minor problems may occur from time to time but these are rare. Continuous Improvement is clearly evident.

10. Continuous Improvement processes ensure sustained performance. Could be used as a benchmark. Excellent supporting documentation that is updated as part of continuous improvement. Consistent application of the requirements of the indicator over time. Based on current industry practices, the assessors cannot identify scope for improvement.

SRM Maturity Models

Security Risk Management Body Of Knowledge (SRMBOK)

The SRMBOK maturity model addresses the following four levels:
1) Level 1 INITIAL
2) Level 2 BASIC
3) Level 3 REPEATABLE
4) Level 4 OPTIMIZING

The model also addresses six categories of maturity:
- Overview
- Culture
- Systems
- Experience
- Training
- Management

Assessment descriptors for each of the categories are outlined below.

Overview

1) Compliance-only approach. Risk appetite is not defined. No framework developed. No senior management support. No use of SRM to inform decision-making
2) SRM established for loss prevention. Shared but poorly articulated SRM tolerance. SRM implemented at lower levels. Few policies and procedures
3) SRM built into routine business processes and management systems. Comprehensive SRM policy and procedures. Benefits recognized at all levels of the organization
4) SRM considered critical to competitive advantage and achievement of objectives. Security risk appetite and approach is documented and promulgated to all levels of the organization. SRM management systems demonstrate continuous improvement. SRM proactive and focused on opportunity realization.

Culture

1) SRM implemented to meet minimum legislated requirements.
2) SRM exposure defined. Roles and responsibilities defined. Basic SRM decision-making mechanisms
3) Proactive approach to SRM. Support for SRM at all levels of the organization. High level security risks reviewed by senior management or board
4) SRM culture is led by the Chief Executive. SRM information is used in decision-making. SRM roles and responsibilities included in inductions, job descriptions and performance appraisals

Systems

1) SRM strategy and management systems non-existent or ad hoc

2) SRM framework under development. BCM and resilience not addressed. Poor data collection and analysis.
3) Strategy and management systems are documented and consistently applied. SRM framework is in place and partially integrated with BCM.
4) SRM framework and management systems are defined and benchmarked against best practice. Continuous improvement is evident at all levels.

Experience
1) Very limited understanding of SRM systems or terminology.
2) Limited to small number of security practitioners.
3) In-house core of experienced individuals, systems and modeling.
4) Organization has in-depth experience at all levels and experiences are analyzed and recorded as part of normal knowledge management processes

Training
1) Training implemented only to the level required by legislation.
2) Training undertaken only by security practitioners.
3) Organizational training needs are analyzed and met. Security training provided to staff at all levels.
4) Training and education programs are based on robust and up-to-date training needs analysis. Relevant training is provided to all levels of the organization.

Management
1) Management practices are focused on meeting legislated requirements. Response to critical incidents is the prime initiator for SRM.
2) SRM management practices are based on organizational

management systems. Majority of SRM is reactive. Security systems are reviewed on an ad hoc basis.

3) Guidance for SRM provided to all levels of management. Resource allocation commensurate with risk. Security plans are reviewed at least annually.

4) Guidance on SRM implementation is provided to all levels of the organization. Lead indicators & benchmarks are established & monitored. Resource allocation is monitored & optimized. SRM is integrated and plans are reviewed & tested at least annually.

Australian Risk Management Capability Maturity Model.

Another risk maturity model worth considering is the Australian Government Commonwealth Risk Management Capability Maturity Model.[1] This model outlines the following levels:

1. Fundamental
2. Developed
3. Systematic
4. Integrated
5. Advanced
6. Optimal

It also provides criteria for measuring them against the following nine elements:

1. Establishing a risk management policy
2. Establishing a risk management framework
3. Defining responsibility for managing risk
4. Embedding systematic risk management into business processes
5. Developing a positive risk culture
6. Communicating and consulting about risk
7. Understanding and managing shared risk
8. Maintaining risk management capability
9. Reviewing and continuously improving the management of risk

Details can be found at:

https://www.finance.gov.au/sites/default/files/commonwealth-risk-management-maturity-model.pdf

Enterprise Security Risk Assessment

Enterprise security risk management (ESRM) includes the methods and processes to manage security risks and realize opportunities related to organizational objectives. ESRM typically involves identifying events or circumstances relevant to the organization's objectives, assessing them, determining a response strategy, and monitoring progress.

Enterprise Security Risk Assessment (ESRA) differs from conventional security risk assessment, not only in scale but also in its nature. A conventional security risk assessment (SRA) seeks to analyze the risks of a business unit or subset of the enterprise (e.g. a particular facility, project, or system).

By contrast, an ESRA has little interest in the specifics of each business unit unless they demonstrate thematic issues that are evident across sections of the enterprise. The focus of an ESRA is on the security of the overall enterprise. It may also seek to establish measures such as security standards, systems, and protocols so that individual units all face similar levels of risks.

You cannot approach and ESRA as an organization that owns or operates (say) 100 offices, 50 servers, and 3 data centers in 20 countries. The concept requires that the security risk analyst(s) must focus on the totality of an integrated enterprise. An enterprise that, operates a single business across many facilities, operates a cloud server, and happens to have a presence in 20 nations.

There should be no requirement to visit each of the countries or even a majority of the locations and systems to conduct an ESRA and develop an enterprise security treatment plan. It is essential however, to understand and evaluate the threats and risks across each level or category of business units.

A scoping statement for an ESRA might include:

- Enterprise-wide strategic security Risks (Physical, Personnel, Technology, and Information).
- Business activities and corporate operations globally.
- Review of enterprise-wide strategic security measures currently in place for the protection of personnel, assets, and information both at our facilities and while in transit.
- Review and develop security standards and postures across a range of threat levels such that the enterprise can respond with established protocols to any variation in threat levels.
- IT systems as well as interfaces with key external systems.
- Physical protection of server rooms and systems.
- Review of existing security policies, procedures, documents, incident reports, manuals, etc.
- Identification of risks associated with key assets, activities, and operations of the organization.
- Identification and assessment of key vulnerabilities and threats.
- Qualitative and quantitative assessment of security risks currently facing the enterprise.
- Recommend treatment plans to manage or mitigate the risk to an acceptable residual level.

SRA Project Brief Headings

Project Brief Headings Example

The following is one example of how to structure a consultants brief or request for quotation to conduct a Security Risk Assessment. You can download a 6 page example and template from www.srmam.com.

1. **EXECUTIVE SUMMARY**
2. **OBJECTIVES**
3. **SCOPE**
4. **CONTEXT**
5. **PROGRAM**
   5.1. Timelines
   5.2. Project Management
   5.3. Project Liaison
   5.4. Conduct of the Project
6. **SECURITY RISK ASSESSMENT**
   6.1. Reference Documents
   6.2. Outcomes
   6.3. Indicative Terms Of Reference
   6.4. Scope, Context, Criteria
   6.5. Methodology
7. **SKILL SET REQUIREMENTS**
   7.1 Mandatory
   7.2 Desirable

8. SUBMISSIONS

8.1. Conflict of Interest

8.2. Legislative Compliance

8.3. Confidentiality

9. EVALUATION CRITERIA

SRA Report Headings

Report Headings Example 1

The following is one example of how to structure a Security Risk Assessment.

TERMS AND DEFINITIONS
TABLE OF CONTENTS
EXECUTIVE SUMMARY
SCOPE, CONTEXT AND CRITERIA
ASSET CRITICALITY ASSESSMENT
THREAT ASSESSMENT
RISK CONTROL EFFECTIVENESS ASSESSMENT
SECURITY RISK REGISTER & TREATMENTS
ANNEX: ASSESSMENT METHODOLOGY
> *Asset Criticality Assessment*
> *Threat Assessment*
> *Risk Control Effectiveness (RCE) Assessment*
> *Risk Assessment*

Report Headings Example 2

The following is an alternative example of a starting point for structuring an enterprise security risk assessment report.

1. EXECUTIVE SUMMARY
   1.1 Findings and Recommendations
   1.2 Key Risks
   1.3 Priority Recommendations

2. INTRODUCTION
   2.1 Objectives
   2.2 Scope
   2.3 References
   2.4 Definitions
   2.5 Methodology

3. BACKGROUND
   3.1 Context
   3.2 Overview of the Organization
   3.3 Stakeholders
   3.4 Security Culture
   3.5 Risk Criteria

4. RISK IDENTIFICATION
   4.1 Assets at Risk
   4.2 Sources of Risk
   4.3 Threat Assessment
   4.4 Vulnerabilities
   4.5 Potential Risk Events
   4.6 Potential Consequences

5. RISK REGISTER

6. RISK TREATMENTS

7. ADDITIONAL FINDINGS
   7.1 Overview

7.2 Findings

7.3 Key Recommendations

7.4 Opportunities for Improvement

8. MONITORING & REVIEW

8.1 Review

8.2 Immediate Monitoring Requirements

8.3 Additional Considerations for Future Review

9. APPENDIX 1: SECURITY PLAN

Security Plan Headings

Security Plan Headings Example

The following is one example of how to structure a Security Plan. You can download a template from www.srmam.com.

Note: Plans may differ based on the focus and nature i.e. whilst an event security plan and a critical infrastructure protection plan will be underpinned by the same principles they may be significantly different in layout, focus, and even approach.

See also: Treatment Plans and Documenting Complex Treatments in PART C: ADDITIONAL TOOLS: Risk Treatments.

FOREWORD
INTRODUCTION
Scope
Purpose
References
METHODOLOGY
Developing the Plan
Security Threats
Security Risks
Security Strategies
Budget and Funding
Actionable Items

Key Result Areas
Key Performance Indicators
Links to Other Security Plans
Unit and Workgroup Security Plan Development
Security Plan Preparation Checklist
MONITORING AND REVIEW
ENTERPRISE SECURITY PLAN SUMMARY
ANNEX A - SECURITY TREATMENT WORKSHEETS

PART C: ADDITIONAL TOOLS

Monte Carlo Simulation

Monte Carlo simulation (also called the Monte Carlo Method or Monte Carlo sampling) is a a complex but important topic for risk assessment. It is a way to account for risk in decision making and quantitative analysis. The method involves running hundreds or thousands of simulations to develop a range of probable outcomes.

The result is usually a graph or probability distribution curve which shows the likelihood of various consequences.

It was invented during the Manhattan Project by John von Neumann and Stanislaw Ulam and named in recognition of the games of chance in Monte Carlo, Monaco.

You can find Monte Carlo tools and more information about how it works in Excel in 'How to Measure Anything in Cybersecurity Risk'[1] as well as from Microsoft[2] and suppliers such as:

- Palisade[3]
- RiskAmp[4]
- Analytica[5]

Ishikawa Diagrams

Ishikawa diagrams (also called fishbone diagrams, herringbone diagrams, cause-and-effect diagrams, or Fishikawa) are causal diagrams created by Kaoru Ishikawa that show the causes of a specific event or potential event.

PART C: ADDITIONAL TOOLS

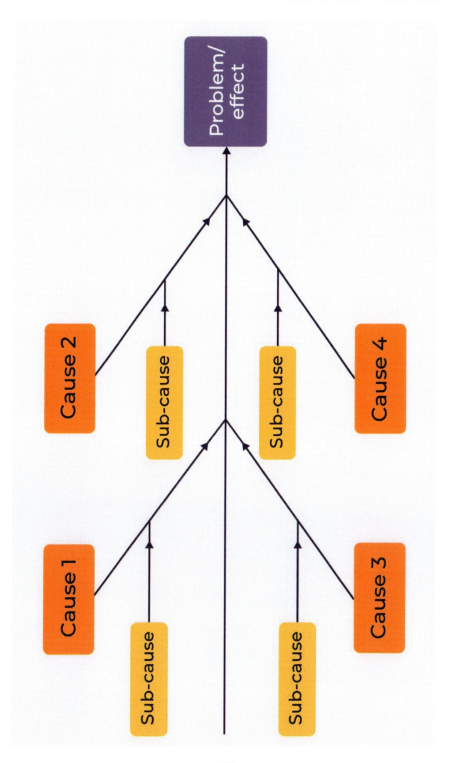

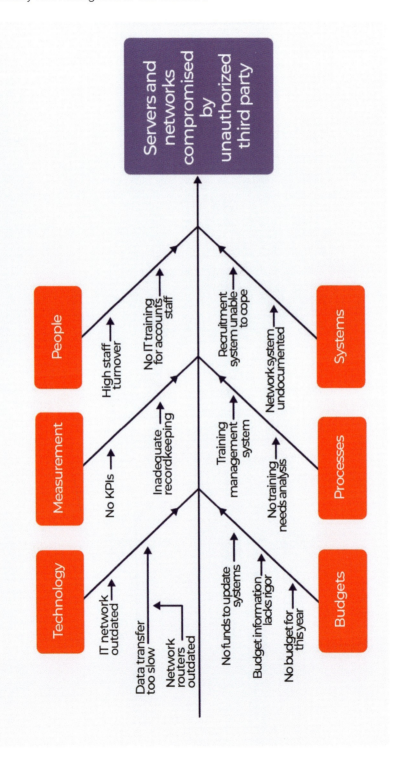

PART C: ADDITIONAL TOOLS

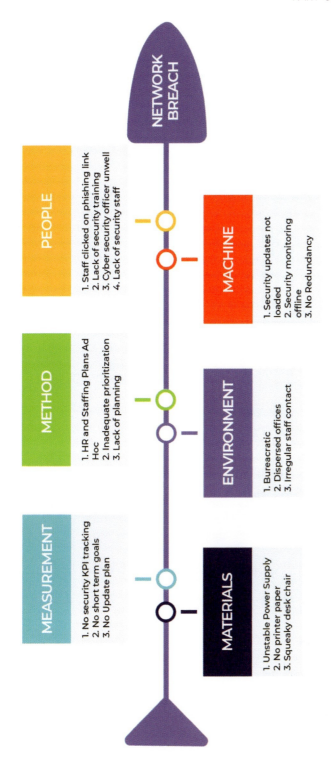

Attack Trees

Attack trees are conceptual diagrams showing how an asset, or target, might be attacked. The following graphic is adapted from Bruce Schneier's website and his 1999 article 'Attack Trees'.[1]

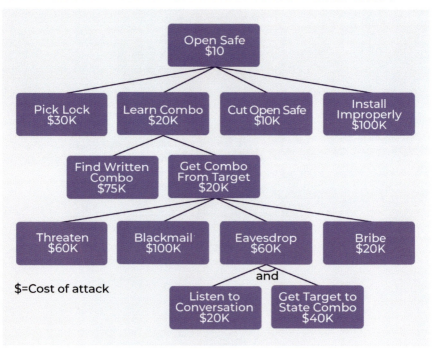

PART D: MODELS AND FRAMEWORKS

Definitions

Definitions

These definitions are not comprehensive. Please consider them simply as brief clarifications to indicate their use in this booklet. Unless otherwise stated, they are adapted from longer definitions in ISO31000 or SRMBOK. Any terms you come across in the book that are new to you can be found in one of these two documents.

If you do not have access to the above resources, most dictionaries will be adequate. The CISSP Glossary is also a easily accessible list of excellent security definitions. It differs from SRMBOK or ISO31000 in some respects but covers a lot of ground and is generally consistent with the way definitions have been used in this document. https://www.isc2.org/Certifications/CISSP/CISSP-Student-Glossary

Assets

a.k.a. Resources. They can be both the target of an attack and the means for defending against it. NB. ISO31000 refers to Resources rather than Assets.

Attack Vector

The type of event, method or means of attack

Consequences

The outcome of an event which affects the company's objectives. Measured in terms of impact on objectives, resources, assets, capability, or any other metric determined in the risk criteria. For negative consequences, that includes adverse impacts, terms like shock, etc. Positive consequences are benefits.

Controls

Process, policy, device, or other action that acts to minimize negative risk or enhance positive opportunities.

Event

Threat Act, incident, attack, etc.

Exposure

a.k.a. Attack surface. Time frame, duration, frequency, or points of potential attack (virtual or physical) in which an asset is exposed to potential threats or opportunities, e.g. for a home, this might include doors, windows, roof, as well as internet ingress, computer terminals, etc.

Hazard

Inanimate potential source of harm.

Likelihood

Chance, Frequency, Probability

Risk

The effect of uncertainty on objectives

Source

a.k.a. Threat. Person or thing which could initiate an attack or release of a hazard by deliberate actions. For positive risks, it means opportunity.

Vulnerability

Weakness that can be exploited by an adversary to gain access to an asset.

ISO31000 Risk Management Standard

ISO31000 Principles

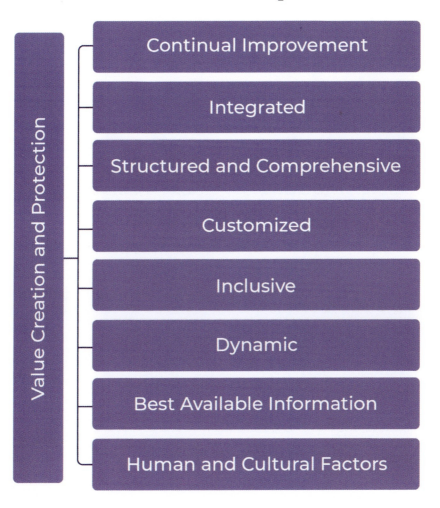

ISO31000 Framework

ISO31000 Process

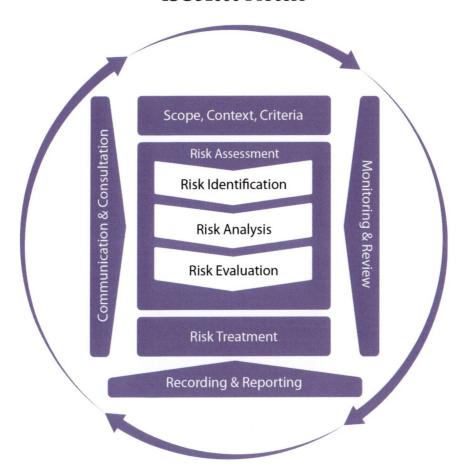

SRMBOK Framework

The following Framework graphics have been adapted from the SRMBOK organizational resilience model in SRMBOK (FIGURE 11.2). The main change is to simplify the diagram and establish Objectives rather than Capability as the key outcome.

PART D: MODELS AND FRAMEWORKS

OBJECTIVES

Capabilities

SECURITY IN DEPTH (ESIEAP)

KNOWLEDGE AREAS
Exposure, Risk, Resource, Quality

SRM INTEGRATION

COMPETENCY AREAS
Integration, Design, Application, Assurance

ACTIVITY AREAS
Intelligence, Security, Response, Recovery

PRACTICE AREAS
Security Management, Physical, Information, People, ICT

ENABLERS
Regulation, Training, Operations, Governance, Sustainability

Security-in-depth provides layers of protection to protect resources, in order to sustain capability. The purpose of capability however is to support achievement of objectives.

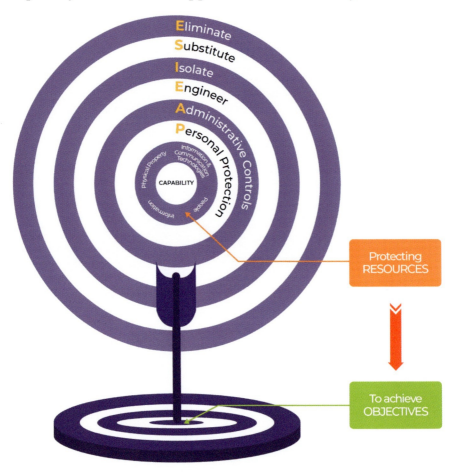

The following graphic illustrates one way of structuring a security risk management system (SRMS).

PART D: MODELS AND FRAMEWORKS

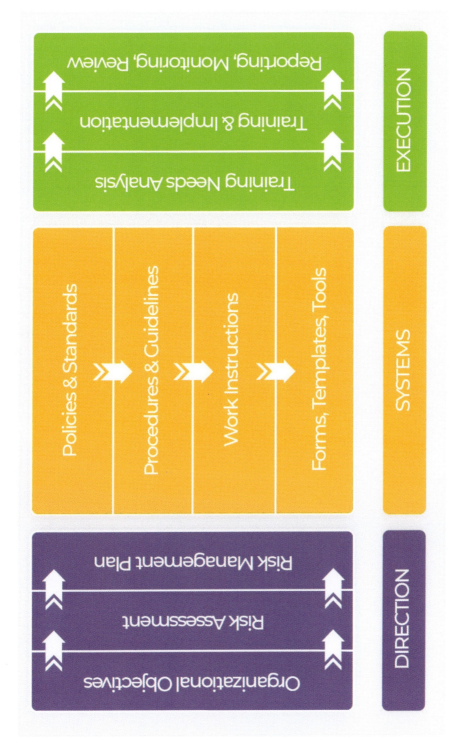

SRMBOK Methodology

This methodology has minor adaptations from *'FIGURE 11.3 Expansion of AS/NZS 4360:2004 Risk Management Process for Security Risk Management'* in SRMBOK (2009) to reflect the updates to ISO31000:2018.

Individual elements are described in more detail in this Aide-Memoire at Threat Assessment, Vulnerability Analysis, Criticality Assessment and Risk Treatments.

This model is not necessarily the best or only model. Nor does it need to be followed in a step by step process. It is designed purely to illustrate the relationships of various elements of security risk assessment to each other and provide a level of integration with models such as CARVER, ISO31000 Process, and Hierarchy of Controls in a single diagram.

It is available for download from www.srmam.com.

PART D: MODELS AND FRAMEWORKS

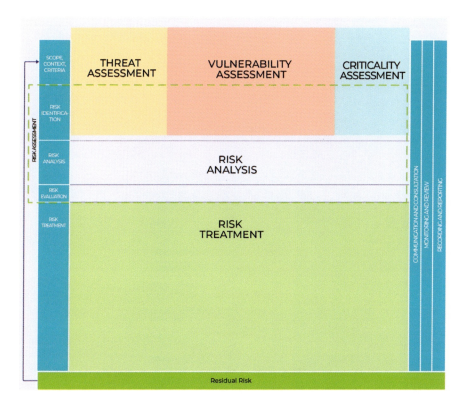

Security Risk Management Aide-Memoire

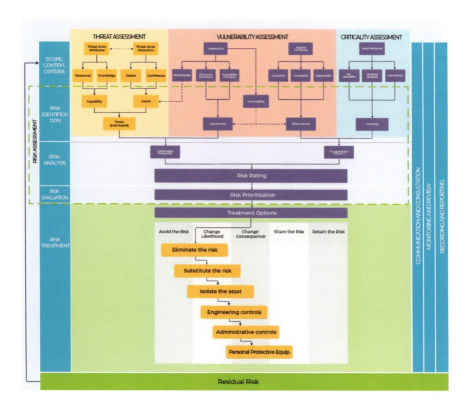

Other Security Frameworks

Security Frameworks

The following is a partial list of sources for security-related frameworks. Their presence here is not an endorsement, just a resource if you are looking for more references. I have not included links for forward-compatibility reasons, but an online search will reveal their latest incarnations.

- ANSI
- Australian Government Protective Security Policy Framework (PSPF)
- CIS v7
- CISQ
- Control Objectives for Information and Related Technologies (COBIT)
- COSO
- FedRAMP
- FISMA
- GDPR
- HB167 Security Handbook
- HIPAA
- HITRUST CSF
- How to mitigate cyber security incidents (Australian Cyber Security Centre; Australian Signals Directorate)
- IASME Governance
- IRAP

- NERC CIP
- NIST 800-53
- NIST Cybersecurity Framework
- NIST SP 800-12
- NIST SP 800-14
- NIST SP 800-16
- NY DFS
- SCAP
- SOC 2
- TC CYBER
- Ten Steps to Cybersecurity (UK National Cyber Security Centre, GCHQ)
- UK HMG Security Policy Framework

PART E: REFERENCES

Most of the material in this book is based on:
- Security Risk Management Body of Knowledge (SRMBOK)
- ISO31000:2018 Risk Management Standard (ISO31000)

Some additional references include:
- Control Objectives for Information and related Technologies (COBIT) describes common requirements organizations should have in place around information systems.
- Standards Australia HB 167 Security Risk Management provides coverage of security risk management and assessment tools and techniques.
- The International Organization for Standardization (ISO) also publish many standards related to risk management and security including:
  - ISO 27001 describes an approach for setting up an information security management system.
  - ISO 27002 goes into more detail on the specifics of ISO 27005 Information Technology - Security Techniques - Information Security Risk Management
  - ISO 27005 Information Technology - Security Techniques - Information Security Risk Management
  - ISO 28000:2007 Specification for security management systems for the supply chain

Newsletters

Some of the security newsletters which can be helpful in staying up to date:

- Australian Cyber Security Centre https://www.cyber.gov.au/news
- Julian Talbot https://www.juliantalbot.com/paper-li
- Pentest Magazine https://pentestmag.com
- Schneier on Security https://www.schneier.com/crypto-gram/subscribe.html
- Security Management Daily, ASIS Online www.asisonline.org
- Security Newsletter https://securitynewsletter.co
- The Hacker News https://thehackernews.com
- ThreatPost https://threatpost.com

Each day (at least in 2019) I also post some articles I find interesting at Linkedin bit.ly/InterestingArticles They aren't all about security but are whatever I find interesting at the time. They are typically about technology, artificial intelligence, security, privacy, risk management, travel, financial markets, and investing.

PART E: REFERENCES

Online Resources

- Australian Cyber Security Centre www.cyber.gov.au
- Australian Attorney-General's Department www.protectivesecurity.gov.au
- Australian Critical Infrastructure Centre www.homeaffairs.gov.au/about-us/our-portfolios/national-security/security-coordination/critical-infrastructure-resilience
- Australian Government Risk Resources www.finance.gov.au/risk-resources/
- Australian Trusted Information Sharing Network (TISN) www.tisn.gov.au
- US CISA www.us-cert.gov
- European Union Agency For CyberSecurity www.enisa.europa.eu/topics
- OWASP Foundation www.owasp.org
- UK National Cyber Security Centre www.ncsc.gov.uk
- UK Centre for the Protection of National Infrastructure www.cpni.gov.uk
- US Department of Homeland Security www.dhs.gov/science-and-technology/cybersecurity
- US DoD Cyber Exchange public.cyber.mil
- US National Institute of Standards and Technology www.nist.gov/topics/cybersecurity
- US National Security Agency www.nsa.gov/what-we-do/cybersecurity
- US Office of Personnel Management www.opm.gov/cybersecurity

Software

While MS Excel has long been the go-to tool for creating security risk assessments, there are many alternatives. A friend and I have been working on a recently released Software-as-a-Service (SaaS) security risk assessment product which allows users to create professional and methodologically rigorous assessments, with all the benefits you would expect of a collaborative, secure and productivity-inducing platform.

SECTARA was developed by leading security risk practitioner Konrad Buczynski and his team, with myself having an ongoing level of involvement and interest. SECTARA puts into action SRMBOK concepts, in a way that makes it very easy. Try out the free plan at your leisure (https://sectara.com/free-plan).

If you're loyal to MS Excel, you can also check out my website at www.juliantalbot.com for several free templates.

If You Like This Book

If you enjoyed this book, I'd appreciate it if you could let the world know by going to Amazon or Goodreads and leaving a review. I, and future readers, will be grateful for the time you take to do this.

- Amazon.com
- Amazon.com.au
- Amazon.co.uk
- Amazon.de
- Amazon.fr
- Amazon.es
- Amazon.co.jp

Thanks for your help in getting the word out. I hope the book is useful for you. If you have any questions, or suggestions for future editions, please drop me a line via www.juliatalbot.com or post on the discussion forum at www.srmam.com.

About the Author

Julian Talbot has written and co-authored several books including the Security Risk Management Body Of Knowledge (SRMBOK). He is a Fellow of the Risk Management Institute of Australasia, recipient of The Australian Security Medal, and has a Master of Risk Management degree.

His experience includes Manager of Property and Security for the Australian government's most extensive international network (the Australian Trade Commission), Manager of Security for Australia's largest natural resources project (Woodside's $24 billion NW Shelf Venture), Operations Manager for IMX Resources' East African Exploration operations, Senior Risk Adviser for the $30 billion Australian Department of Health & Ageing, and Head of Security and Risk for Malaysian Smelting Corporation's Indonesian operations.

Julian has also held several roles as Company Director, Risk Management Practice Leader and later CEO of the $30 million Jakeman Business Solutions, and Divisional Manager (People & Advisory Division) of the $240 million ASX listed Citadel Group Limited.

He enjoys working with startups, time with family and friends, motorcycling, and travel (especially to places which have a travel advisory warning). He is also strangely compelled to write but blessed with optimism bias when it comes to estimating how long a book will take.

Endnotes

Swiss-Cheese

1. Reason, James. *Human Error*. 1 edition. Cambridge England; New York: Cambridge University Press, 1990.

Heuristics and Biases

1. 'Essays: The Psychology of Security (Part 1) - Schneier on Security'. Accessed 22 October 2019. https://www.schneier.com/essays/archives/2008/01/the_psychology_of_se.html.
2. 'List of Cognitive Biases'. In *Wikipedia*, 18 October 2019. https://en.wikipedia.org/w/index.php?title=List_of_cognitive_biases&oldid=921897950.
3. Kahneman, Daniel. *Thinking, Fast and Slow*. 1 edition. New York: Farrar, Straus and Giroux, 2011.

Situational Awareness

1. Schneider, Gavriel. *Can I See Your Hands: A Guide To Situational Awareness, Personal Risk Management, Resilience and Security*. Irvine: Universal Publishers, 2017.

HFACS

1. Department of Defense. 'Human Factors Analysis and Classification System'. Department of Defense, 2005. https://www.public.navy.mil/NAVSAFECEN/Documents/WESS/DOD%20HFACS.PDF.
2. Reason, James. *Human Error*. 1 edition. Cambridge England; New York: Cambridge University Press, 1990.

Risk Tolerance

1. Finance, Department of. 'Risk Resources'. Text, 22 August 2017. https://www.finance.gov.au/risk-resources/.

* * *

SCAP

1. Computer Security Division, Information Technology Laboratory. 'Security Content Automation Protocol | CSRC'. CSRC | NIST, 7 December 2016. https://csrc.nist.gov/projects/security-content-automation-protocol/.
2. 'Home | OpenSCAP Portal'. Accessed 5 September 2019. https://www.open-scap.org/.

STRIDE

1. 'STRIDE (Security)'. In *Wikipedia*, 29 September 2019. https://en.wikipedia.org/w/index.php?title=STRIDE_(security)&oldid=918601029.

Analysis of Competing Hypotheses

1. Heuer, Richards J. *Psychology of Intelligence Analysis*. 1st ed. Vol. Chapter 8 — Central Intelligence Agency, 2007. https://www.cia.gov/library/center-for-the-study-of-intelligence/csi-publications/books-and-monographs/psychology-of-intelligence-analysis/art11.html.

Vulnerability Analysis

1. Nutrition, Center for Food Safety and Applied. 'CARVER + Shock Primer'. FDA, 19 March 2019. http://www.fda.gov/food/food-defense-programs/carver-shock-primer.
2. Caralli, Richard A., James F. Stevens, Lisa R. Young, and William R. Wilson. 'Introducing OCTAVE Allegro: Improving the Information Security Risk Assessment Process': Fort Belvoir, VA: Defense Technical Information Center, 1 May 2007. https://doi.org/10.21236/ADA470450.

Risk Estimation

1. Tetlock, Philip E. *Expert Political Judgment: How Good Is It? How Can We Know?* New Ed edition. Princeton, N.J.: Princeton University Press, 2006.
2. Hubbard, Douglas W., and Richard Seiersen. *How to Measure Anything in Cybersecurity Risk*. Hoboken: Wiley, 2016.
3. Thomas, Philip, Reidar Bratvold, and J.Eric BIckel. 'The Risk of Using Risk Matrices'. New Orleans, 2013. https://www.researchgate.net/publication/259640343_The_Risk_of_Using_Risk_Matrices.

* * *

Risk Matrices

1. Cox, Tony. 'What's Wrong with Risk Matrices?' Risk Analysis, 1 April 2008. https://onlinelibrary.wiley.com/doi/abs/10.1111/j.1539-6924.2008.01030.x.
2. Talbot, Julian. 'What's Right with Risk Matrices?' juliantalbot. Accessed 7 July 2019. https://www.juliantalbot.com/post/2018/07/31/whats-right-with-risk-matrices.
3. Hillson, David. 'Extending the Risk Process to Manage Opportunities', 2002. /paper/Extending-the-risk-process-to-manage-opportunities-Hillson/94a79f3515676ffa2474cf7a2b36024a81fb904f.

Stroud Matrix

1. Taleb, Nassim Nicholas. *The Black Swan: Second Edition: The Impact of the Highly Improbable: With a New Section: 'On Robustness and Fragility'*. 2 edition. New York: Random House Trade Paperbacks, 2010.

Risk Expectancy

1. Hubbard, Douglas W., and Richard Seiersen. *How to Measure Anything in Cybersecurity Risk*. Hoboken: Wiley, 2016.

AusGov Risk Maturity Model

1. 'Commonwealth Risk Management Capability Maturity Model'. Accessed 22 October 2019. https://www.finance.gov.au/sites/default/files/commonwealth-risk-management-maturity-model-one-pager.pdf.

Monte Carlo Simulation

1. Hubbard, Douglas W., Richard Seiersen, Daniel E. Geer Jr., and Stuart McClure. *How to Measure Anything in Cybersecurity Risk*. 1 edition. Hoboken: Wiley, 2016.
2. https://support.office.com/en-us/article/Introduction-to-Monte-Carlo-simulation-in-Excel-64c0ba99-752a-4fa8-bbd3-4450d8db16f1
3. Palisade. 'What Is Monte Carlo Simulation?' Monte Carlo Simulation: What Is It and How Does It Work? - Palisade. Accessed 12 August 2019. https://www.palisade.com/risk/monte_carlo_simulation.asp.
4. 'What Is Monte Carlo Simulation.Pdf'. Accessed 12 August 2019. https://www.riskamp.com/files/RiskAMP%20-%20Monte%20Carlo%20Simulation.pdf.
5. Analytica. 'Monte Carlo Simulation'. Accessed 22 October 2019. https://analytica.com/technology/monte-carlo-simulation-software/.

* * *

Attack Trees

[1] 'Academic: Attack Trees - Schneier on Security'. Accessed 5 September 2019. https://www.schneier.com/academic/archives/1999/12/attack_trees.html.

Printed by Amazon Italia Logistica S.r.l.
Torrazza Piemonte (TO), Italy